1 MONTH OF
FREE
READING

at

www.ForgottenBooks.com

By purchasing this book you are eligible for one month membership to ForgottenBooks.com, giving you unlimited access to our entire collection of over 1,000,000 titles via our web site and mobile apps.

To claim your free month visit:

www.forgottenbooks.com/free916458

ISBN 978-0-266-96442-1
PIBN 10916458

This book is a reproduction of an important historical work. Forgotten Books uses
state-of-the-art technology to digitally reconstruct the work, preserving the original format
whilst repairing imperfections present in the aged copy. In rare cases, an imperfection in
the original, such as a blemish or missing page, may be replicated in our edition. We do,
however, repair the vast majority of imperfections successfully; any imperfections that
remain are intentionally left to preserve the state of such historical works.

Pearl River
Community College

Station A Box 155
Poplarville, MS
39470-2298
(601) 795-6801

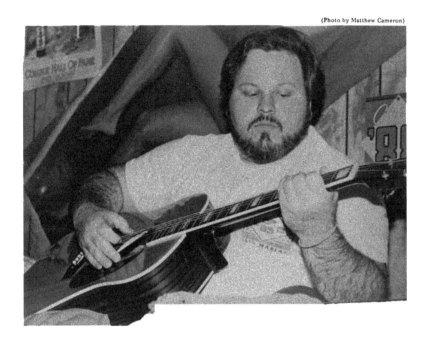

PRC students fill out their forms for the February blood drive.

Michael Seal and Steve Bounds enjoy a good checker game.

Tiffany Early works on the annual.

Republican Convention 1988

George Bush's march to the White House began only 80 miles from the Pearl River campus, with the Republican National Convention in New Orleans Aug. 15-18.

Bush and running mate Dan Quayle cruised to victory over Democratic opponent Michael Dukakis and his vice-presidential nominee George Bensten.

The Republicans won the electorial vote race handily, gathering 426 to 112. They also got 47,946,422 popular votes to the Democrat's 41,016,429.

In Mississippi 58.4 percent of the state's estimated 1.59 million voters (932,000) turned out for the election. Bush and Quayle got 60 percent of the popular vote with 552,879. Dukakis and Bensten got 362,298, 39 percent.

In the Senate race Republican Trent Lott got 54 percent of the vote to take the victory over Democrat Wayne Dowdy.

According to information released at the convention, the Republican Party spent $9,200,000 on the event, which was held at the Louisiana Superdome. The funding came from the Federal Elections

Commission, which gave equal sums to both parties for their conventions.

The Convention was expected to draw as many as 45,000 visitors, 15,000 media personnel, 2,277 delegates and an equal number of alternates to the city, which had to chip in with $6 million to cover the cost of leasing the Dome, providing security and other services.

Equipment for the event included 4,000 telephones, 175 miles of cable, 1.2 million pounds of scaffolding, and 150,000 nuts and bolts.

The area around the convention center was a definite eye catcher.

More than 150,000 balloons were used to decorate the Dome.

(Photos by James Stewart)

Elephants abounded in New Orleans during the convention.

Christina Hatten, above, dances at a pep rally.

Band members perform at a home game.

"We've got spirit . . ."

Rina Roberson, below, performs at the Jones pep rally.

W.C. Rivers cats around at another pep rally.

'We've got more   ''

Fall Registration 1988

Dr. John Grant, left, and Bill Kirkpatrick, center, share a Coke during registration.

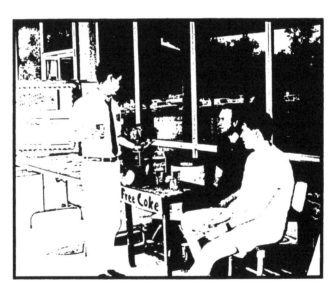

10

Students fight lines to get classes.

Eva Henry, right, and a friend leave the gym following student orientation.

BREAK TIME

The Pearls perform at a weekly pep rally.

David Bowls lounges around after band practice.

A pair of PRC students take their cat for a stroll.

A group of band students clown around after practice.

Jeff Thompson shows his muscle.

Treasures

of the

River

Student Life

Angela McIntyre, Traci Selman, Angela Smith, Nancy McBrice (back row), Kristi Cole, Jennifer Hyatt and Lynn Seal celebrate a birthday.

A group of guys attend a pep rally.

Ceci Douglas performs with the Pearls.

Tanis Breland and *Robin Seal* pose for a photo.

Eric Favre, Jamie Favre and Mike Raphael goofing off in Marion Hall.

Toni Mitchell and *Tonya Foil in their room.*

Sherri Campbell and Sherri Carver take a break
from cheering to pose for a picture.

David Stromeyer gets fired-up for football game.

Paula Magee performs during half-time.

A P.R.C. student takes a break between classes.

Fara Bailey and Roxanne Wise *stop off on their way to lunch.*

Arthur Wynne and Greg Pritchett *scope out Marion Hall.*

Britt Wood takes a break between classes.

P.R.C. students wait in lunch line.

Julie Powell on her way downstairs in Marion Hall.

Homecoming celebration ruled a success

No matter how you measure it Pearl River's 1988 Homecoming celebration was a success.

"I thought it was fantastic," Donna Wilson, director of the Development Foundation and Alumni Affairs office, said. "I thought it was the most successful we've ever had."

She said 425 alumni were on hand at the annual luncheon in the M.R. White Coliseum, 55 more than 1987's total, adding that all of the comments she received about the festivities were favorable.

Pearl River County received the award for having the most people in attendance with 112.

And Howard Willoughby of Cedar Grove was named the Alumni of the Year, while Herchel and Ruby Bullock of Bakersfield, Ca., received an award for traveling the farthest, 1,960 miles.

Sherrie Campbell of Purvis reigned as queen during the game, while her court included sophomore maids April Austin, Angela Haddox and Jennifer Hyatt, freshman maids Beverly Cagins, Sherri Carver and Mary Henry, and football maids Leigh Morris and Karen Irvin.

Phi Beta Lambda, a business society, took first place in the campus display contest, and VICA took second.

Other clubs participating in the contest included the Afro-American Cultural Society, Baptist Student Union, Delta Psi Omega, Mississippi Student Nurses Association, Phi Theta Kappa, PRC Cheerleaders, Cosmo, Forrest County Respiratory Therapy, DECA and the Wesley Foundation.

Queen
Sherrie Campbell

20

April Austin
Sophomore Maid

Angela Haddox
Sophomore Maid

Jennifer Hyatt
Sophomore Maid

Karen Irvin
Football Maid

Leigh Morris
Football Maid

Beverly Cagins
Freshman Maid

Sherri Carver
Freshman Maid

Mary Jane Henry
Freshman Maid

(Photo by James Stewart)

Sophomore maid Jennifer Hyatt entertains a guest during the first half of the game.

Darla Daniels, Stuart Fore and Mike Simms film homecoming activities.

Dr. Marvin R. White, former PRC president (below), greets visitors at the luncheon.

Queen Sherrie Campbell, escorted by her father Billy D. Campbell (left), receives a bouquet of roses from Larry Tynes and Dr. Ted Alexander.

W.C. Rivers offers a Homecoming greeting to the queen.

Rhonda Reid, president of Phi Lambda Delta, accepts her club's first place award in the display contest.

Donna Wilson, left, presents VICA officers Candy Emerick and Bobby Rushing with their club's second place award in the display contest.

The Homecoming Court, below, watches the start of the game with their escorts.

A band student performs during halftime.

Sonya McRaney reacts to a quarterback sack.

Mike Raphael, Sammy McCardle and Kit Vizzini sit in Marion Hall after lunch.

Two students chat before class.

Nadi Davis finds humor in a

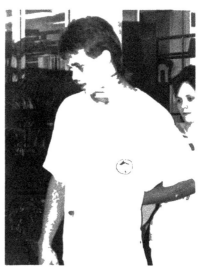

Nazli Davis finds humor in scrubbing the carpet.

A student waits in a registration line.

Eddie Bourgeois and Kyle Ward wave at the camera from the stands.

Students clown around between classes.

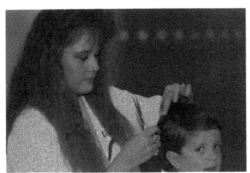

Sonya Smith experiments on child's hair.

Drafting students work on class projects at vo-tech center.

Ben Foxworth walks across blind.

Leslie Ladner watches television.

P.R.C. water tower is a familiar landmark.

Gina Goudy studies in between classes.

Rico Foxworth walks across campus with a friend.

Julie Ferrill practices for the band.

*Todd **Russell**, Mike Weems, Jason Roland, Steven Barrett and Kevin Ladner attend an assembly.*

*Heidi **Austin** poses in the music room.*

*Mark **Necaise** and Jill Dodd chat in Marion Hall.*

A group of students wait in registration line.

Stuart Fore films a rainy football game.

Sherrie Campbell cheers during a football game.

Two students study on a bench during lunch.

Students walk toward their next class.

This student uses his umbrella to block the sun.

Aaron White poses with his friends.

Aaron White and a friend stop for a picture.

A group of students gather near Marion Hall.

A student takes a breather on the Marion Hall steps.

Lou Thomas, Chris Cagle, Mike Byrd and Dave Lee just clowning around.

(Photo by Tiffany Early)

Chris Schaefer, John Atwood, Greg Pritchett and Arthur Wynne hanging out.

(Photo by Teresa Jones)

Angela Haddox says, "You've got to be kidding!"

Marie Stevens checks out Kim Landrum at the P.R.C. Bookstore.

Tricia Glass and April Austin stroll across campus.

Perk Week

Eillen Wynne and *Linda Reid show the results of the shaving creme fight.*

Perk Week bonfire and pep rally.

Perk Week dance

Dana Dearman, *Fara Bailey and Michele Harbeson after shaving creme fight.*

Students in Marion Hall show their River spirit.

Perk Week dance

PRC students observe the ci...

Kristy Clark and Rhonda Bilbo rambo-ing around.

Rhonda Bilbo, Stacey Johnson and Greg Ladner take a break from shaving creme war.

Park Week dance

P.R.C. students observe the cheerleader's new dance.

W.C. Rivers cutting around at pep rally.

Stormy Weather

The **Broadwater Beach Marina** emptied in preparation for Hurricane Florence, the first of two storms to threaten the Mississippi Coast.

(Photos by Stuart Fore)

Workers at the Broadwater Beach Hotel board up as Florence nears. The hurricane hit the coast, but did relatively little damage.

(Photos by Stuart Fore)

These Mississippi residents prepare to take their boat to higher ground. Hurricane Gilbert also threatened the Mississippi Gulf Coast, but veered west and did heavy damage to the Carribean.

These PRC students (from left) Darlene Minton, David Stromeyer, Christina Hatten, Matthew Cameron, Chuck Harrison, Mike Byrd and Rebecca Wood, did not let the weather dampen their spirits. It just gave them a reason to throw a costume party.

Darla Daniels cheers during football game.

Chris Bates eats lunch.

The cheerleaders make a tower.

The Pearls performing during half-time.

The cheerleaders make a tower during a pep rally.

Melanie McNabb performs with the Pearls.

Vicki Seligman sits in deep thought as she helps with registration.

Greg Necaise and Mike Weems fool around before practice.

Keith Hutchens, Darla Daniels and Angela Haddox take refuge under umbrellas during a rainy game.

Jackie Lawrence smiles for the camera.

The football team shows its spirit during a pep rally.

Janice Pucheu attends a pep rally.

Kristy Clark, Wendy Deben and Devin Rose enjoy a football game.

These two students enjoy a warm fall day.

Rina Roberson gets the crowd perked up at a pep rally.

Smokers asked to cut it out in Smokeout

A *helper* with the smokeout fills balloons.

(Photos by James Stewart)

Another helper hands out stickers that say, "Kiss me, I don't smoke."

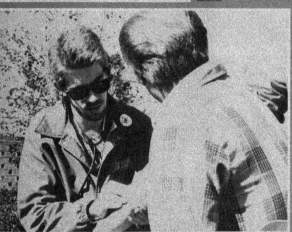

Student body president Terry Ezell (right) shouts encouragement for people to get involved in the smokeout.

Chuck Slater, a nursing student from Picayune, administers a blood pressure test.

Angela Haynes, a business administration major from Hattiesburg, carries a sign asking people to give up smoking.

49

Toys take over Christmas:
A children's play

Ques Stringer, left, and Rich Smith wear the remains of their makeup following a performance.

Vicki Piper pauses for pictures in her costume as Sunny, a doll, in the Christmas children's play.

(Photos by Matthew Cameron)

Some children, left, visit with Santa (Rich Smith). The crew held several shows for local grade-school groups.

Below the toys examine their imprisoned hearts, which prevents them from feeling.

The cast, at bottom, gathers after a show.

Extravaganza worth the planning

Seven months of planning and preparation paid off for Pearl River Community College's Development Foundation, as 350 people were on hand for The River Extravaganza at the end of the spring '88 semester.

"We were very pleased with the turnout," said Donna Wilson, executive director of the development foundation, which sponsored the fund-raising event.

Committee members sold 365 tickets for the Extravaganza which featured entertainment by Jerry Clower, music by local band Dealer's Choice, a food fest and an auction.

Wilson explained that as this was the school's pioneer effort at this type of fund-raiser, many local residents did not know what to expect.

"Not knowing what it was," she said, "people waited until the last minute to buy their advanced tickets."

She added that those who purchased tickets will be sent written invitations before tickets go on sale to the general public for future Extravaganzas.

Wilson said she used the same approach during her two years as foundation director at Southeastern Louisiana University, which has been hosting a similar fund-raising activity for the past four years.

She added that based on the comments her office has received from those who attended The Extravaganza, the foundation should have little trouble reaching future attendance goals.

"Most of the people were here initially because they wanted to help the college," she said. "Now people also know The Extravaganza means good food and a good time.

"This kind of thing is fun for the people involved," she said.

Lisa Henley, a marketing major from Carriere and one of the student workers who helped put the project together, said, "I was really impressed with it. I know the people really enjoyed the food," she added.

Nine area restaurants, along with employees from the school's cafeteria, participated in this year's food fest, and Wilson said she hopes the food fest will become The Extravaganza's main attraction, with as many as 15 participating restaurants.

She also anticipates the auction continuing to play a major role in future Extravaganzas.

The auction went even better than planned, with auction items generating as much as 60 percent of retail value, while Extravaganza planners were told they could only expect to get between 40 and 50 percent of retail value.

Wilson said she was surprised that many of the smaller-ticket items did not go over as well as the more expensive ones.

"I'm looking forward to next year," Henley said.

These ladies face a difficult decision choosing from the many dishes available for tasting at the food fest. Local restaurants prepared everything from baked beans and barbeque, to spicy Cajun seafood dishes and strips of steak.

Shirley Stockman, business office secretary, and Connie Holmes, speech instructor, finish up a snack as they listen to Dealer's Choice, a local band featuring the talents of PRC bandleader Archie Rawls.

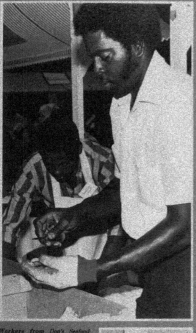

Jerry Clower, Grand Ole Opry comedian from Yazoo City, delivers his monologue to the crowd. Among the anecdotes he told the audience was his trademark tale of "The Coon Hunt."

Miller Hammill, dean of student affairs, and his wife Norma, biology instructor, find a seat in the stands at the M.R. White Coliseum to eat their meal. With restaurant booths and the bandstand dominating the floor space within the coliseum, seating on the ground level was limited, but that did not stop anyone from enjoying the food.

Workers from Don's Seafood Restaurant prepare oysters to be served on the half shell. Don's was one of nine area restaurants participating in the food fest portion of the Extravaganza.

John "Chappy" Chapman, restaurant owner and chef from Biloxi, cooks up a batch of blackened fish. Seafood enthusiast at the Extravaganza could sample from offerings including blackened fish, along with fried oysters and catfish or shrimp salad.

Bubba heads over to put up his lunch tray.

Kirk Stenklyft finishes up with lunch.

Marty Pulliam has lunch with a couple of friends.

PRC students dress their burgers for lunch.

PRC student enjoys her lunch with a friend.

Earnistine Bolden helps serve supper.

Jennifer Dosset, Jeannine Oestreich, Stephanie Lawless and Kris Oden' Hal enjoy their lunches.

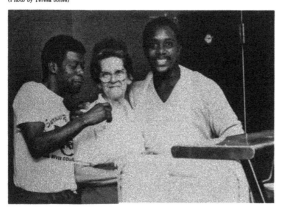

Chip Taylor, Mary Wallace and Ricky Thomas stop work for a minute to clown for the camera.

Melanie McNabb talks to a friend during lunch.

Library: Study,

A group of P.R.C. students wait in line in the library.

Jeanne Slade and Amanda Broom use the library's copy machine.

Homework and Friends

Randy Kippler, Berry McCormick and Billy Fricke chat quietly in the library.

Dennis Devore and Barry Foil discuss a magazine article.

Mike Weems, Bobby Jackson and Britt Woods pose from the balcony of Huff Hall.

Sederick Washington, Jeff Harper and T.J. Davis sit back and relax in between classes.

Bryan Brothers watches T.V. in his room.

Tammy Gipson, Connie Mitchell and Donnie Brothers goof off between classes.

Lisa Warren and *Dawn Patterson* stop outside their dorm to pose for a picture.

Michele Dewease studies in her room for a speech test.

Kristine Odenhal watches t.v. in her dorm.

Jeannine Oestreich and *Stephanie Lawless* show off their dinosaurs.

Jennifer Bailey on her way up to her dorm.

Spring Registration

Kathy Kindred and Linda Reid stop to pose for a picture.

A group of students stand in line waiting to register.

Bookstore workers wait for the next group of students.

Wanda Reddick checks Jeff Harper's name off of the list.

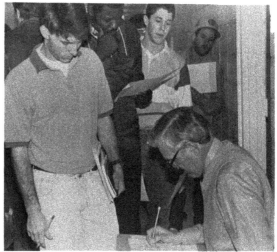

t s picture.

Shonda Davis fills out her registration form.

Mr. Knippers checks over a student's registration form.

d student.

Students wait patiently to register for the spring semester.

Mr. PRC for 1988-89 is Richard
Christopher Schaefer. Chris is the
son of Mr. Richard Schaefer and Mr.
and Mrs. Michael S. Smith of
Lumberton. Chris graduated from
Lumberton High School in 1987 and
is now a sophomore at PRC majoring
in pharmacy. Honors Chris has
received at PRC include an ACT
scholarship, Mr. PRC, Sophomore
Class Vice-President and J.C. scholarship. Chris is a member of the River
Navigators and Phi Theta Kappa.
His hobbies include hunting and
sports.

Terry Ezell
Lumberton

Ruben McDowell
Sumrall

Favorites

Angela Haddox
Picayune

61

Tammy Jenny
Picayune

Chris Cagle
Columbia

Freshman

Chris Lacoste
Bay St. Louis

Greg Ladner
Bay St. Louis

Favorites

Sherrie Carver
Waveland

Stacey Johnson
Petal

Rina Roberson
Bay St. Louis

Who's Who

Cynthia Alexander
Picayune, MS

Marilyn Brant
Foxworth, MS

Kathy Burge
Poplarville, MS

Sean Burns
Bassfield, MS

Martha Byrd
Lumberton, MS

Lisa Carroll
Picayune, MS

Rodney Clark
Hattiesburg, MS

Barbara Cranmer
Bay St. Louis, MS

Keith Creel
McNeill, MS

Doris Dan
Poplarville

Martha Ekor
Picayune, M

Carolyn Geig
Poplarville, M

Who's Who

Darla Daniels
Poplarville, MS

Ceci Douglas
Lumberton, MS

Robert Echols
Lakeshore, MS

Martha Ekornes
Picayune, MS

Julie Ferrill
Poplarville, MS

Anna Gaule
Carriere, MS

Carolyn Geiger
Poplarville, MS

Angela Haddox
Picayune, MS

Cindy Harvey
Picayune, MS

Who's Who

Russell Hendrix
Picayune, MS

Pam Hollensbe
Picayune, MS

Janice Holman
Kokomo, MS

Tammy Jenny
Picayune, MS

Anthony King
Carson, MS

Kim King
Purvis, MS

Margaret Lacavera
Carriere, MS

Jacqueline Lee
Carriere, MS

Berry McCormick
Picayune, MS

Who's Who

Robert McGee
Foxworth, MS

Shirleen Martin
Picayune, MS

Diana Miller
Carriere, MS

Michael Morea
Foxworth, MS

Joseph Napier
Poplarville, MS

Sharon Odom
Picayune, MS

Robert Parish
Sumrall, MS

Rhonda Reid
Lumberton, MS

Todd Russell
Petal, MS

67

Chris Schaffer
Lumberton, MS

Camile Secora
Pass Christian, MS

Drew Smith
Perkinston, MS

Ken Smith
Lumberton, MS

Scott Suhor
Picayune, MS

Mary Thigpen
Picayune, MS

Lee Varnado
Foxworth, MS

Carol Williams
Poplarville, MS

Jack Wooten
Carriere, MS

Not Pictured Are: Dawn Cecil, Patricia Dedeaux, Sheila Smith and Wanda Wagner.

Outstanding

Margaret LaCavera of Carriere and Dr. James Barnes, chairman of the science department, were selected to represent PRC at the Higher Education Appreciation Day - Working for Academic Excellence Program for 1989. LaCavera was named PRC's "Outstanding Student,' and Barnes was named "Outstanding Teacher."

Graduation '88 - A night of firsts

It was a night of firsts at Pearl River Community College's graduation ceremony at the close of the spring 1988 semester.

Not only did the school set a new high with 495 students receiving diplomas or certificates of achievement, it also broke with tradition in having not one, but three commencement speakers.

The speakers were all PRC students, chosen by committee as worthy representatives of their study areas. Shannon Denise Cagle, a business major from Hattiesburg, represented the academic curriculums, while Rochelle Lyn Ledbetter, a medical office technology major from Purvis, was the representative of the technical programs, and Loretta C. Herrin, a nursing major from Sumrall, represented the vocational department.

PRC President Dr. T.J. Alexander said the school had chosen to deviate from the ordinary course of similar events so those who had been able to actually enjoy the opportunities provided by PRC could speak about their experiences.

He said it is important to give students a chance to voice their views, as they are the sole reason for the school's existence.

Cagle, who graduated from Sumrall High School as the salutatorian in 1986, told the audience that, "God gave each one of us here today the potential to be individually special, and it's up to us as individuals to fulfill that potential."

She added that the guidance she received at PRC, both academically and personally, helped her develop her own talents.

Cagle, who held the Elks Club, Lamar County Alumni Association, RiverRoad and Pearl River Singers scholarships, said her stay at PRC represented a move for independence, in that she was away from home for the first time, living in a dorm with 144 other women.

In addition to graduating with a 4.0 average, Cage was a member of the Phi Theta Kappa honor society, RiverRoad showchoir, Pearl River Singers, and String of Pearls dance team. She was also nominated to Who's Who Among American College Students 1987-88 and for the National Collegiate Business Merit Award 1987-88.

Ledbetter told the assembly that upon her graduation in 1986 as Purvis High School's salutatorian, she was looking for junior college training in an interesting career field.

"I found that PRC had what I wanted," she said. "It offered quality education for a reasonable cost and taught skills which are high in demand in the working world of today."

Ledbetter, a 4.0 graduate, who held Pearl River Scholastic and Alumni Scholarships, said the low cost and availability of scholarships, help to limit the expense of a college education.

A member of Phi Theta Kappa, the Baptist Student Union and the Pearl River Singers, she added that campus size is another plus. Students remain important individuals, they do not become mere numbers as on larger campuses.

For Herrin, Sunday's ceremony, at which she graduated with a 4.0 grade point average, was the culmination of a dream come true.

"I know you've all heard that life begins at 40 . . . well, it can, and did for me," she said.

She told the group that while she was not a very motivated student at Purvis High School, where she graduated in 1967, and was busy in the following years starting a family, which includes her husband and son, "I held onto my dream; my dream of becoming a nurse."

Just before her 39th birthday she enrolled in the Practical Nursing Program at PRC to make that dream come true.

And while she graduated with a 4.0 Sunday, Herrin said the program was not a snap, and the completion of her program represented a lot of hard work on her part, and a lot of sacrifice by her family. She said there were many times when family inter-action and household chores had to be set aside in favor of school assignments.

"In spite of the fears, the tears, and the frustrations of starting as a student again after so many years," Herrin said, "I would say to you all, it is never too late, if the dream, the desire, and the will is strong enough. If you want it badly enough . . . go for it! Pearl River will always hold a special place in my heart."

Shannon Cagle delivers her speech.

Loretta Herrin represents the nursing majors.

Rochelle Ledbetter explains what PRC meant to her.

Dr. Joe Kliburn addresses nursing graduates at their pinning ceremony.

Graduating students celebrate at the conclusion of the graduation ceremony, which was held in the Marvin R. White Coliseum.

Above Dr. Ted Alexander awards a diploma and offers congratulations.

At right nursing students take part in the pinning ceremony.

Treasures

of the

River

Sports

Wildcat
Season Record

Opp.	Opponent	PRC
24	Itawamba	22
27	Hinds	27
3	MS Delta	14
14	Jones	31
14	Gulf Coast	21
10	Northeast	3
0	East Central	14
14	Southwest	34
17	Copiah-Lincoln	7
6	Coahoma	33

Brad Greer (55), sophomore from Poplarville, and Will Russell (66), freshman from Mt. Marion, tackle a Bear during the 1989 Homecoming game.

William Earl Harper (32), sophomore from Bassfield, getting tackled during the 1989 Homecoming game with Southwest Junior College.

Greg Nessitt, sophomore from Picayune, gathers together with his friends in the

Practice
Makes Perfect

David Johnston (left) tackles Monwell Magee during one of the practice games before the start of the season.

Coach Bill Martin and Coach Mike Harris review the training schedule while the players work-out in the Wildcat weight room.

Scott Nease looks for an open receiver during some practices on the Wildcat field.

76

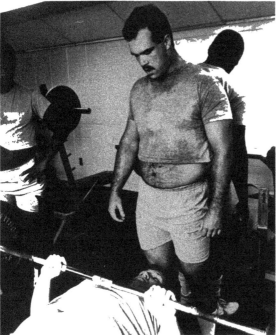

James Philyaw, right, spots for teammate Jason Dugas while improving his physique at the weight bench.

Authur Winne works out in the Wildcat weight room.

Robert McGinty, freshman from Purvis, builds up his muscles before going out to finish up some fierce opponents.

77

WILDCATS

Coaching Staff

Coach *Bill Martin* demonstrates some new blocking techniques to freshman Cedric Washington, of Prentiss, before the start of the season, while freshman Frank Denard, of Hattiesburg, looks on.

1988 Coaching Staff - *front row from left - Student Coach Craig Breland, Defensive Line Coach Bill Martin, Receiver/Defensive Secondary Coach Herbert Morris. Standing from left - Student Coach Darryl Brumfield, Quarterback Coach Jim Nightengale, Wildcat Head Coach Mike Nelson and Offensive Line Coach Mike Harris.*

Wildcat Head Coach, Mike Nelson

1988 Student Management Trainers - *Front row from left - Shannon Davis, Steve Collins, Fred Wrothy. Standing from left - Jeff Davis, Robert Kenny and Woody Adcox.*

Wildcat Trainer, Phil "Doc" Hudson

PRC
Wildcat

When it rains it pours. Even though Roland Johnson (28), Demetric Hall (21) and the rest of the Wildcat team played their best during the first game of the season, they still lost to the Itawamba Indians 24-22.

Head Coach Mike Nelson discusses new playing strategies back Eric Brister during the September 24 game with Jones J which the Wildcats won 31-34.

Marvin Smith (39) grounds a bird during the September 10 tie game with the Hinds Junior College Eagles.

Malter Scoble (96) kicks a field goal during the September 17 MS Delta game which the Wildcats won 14-3.

W.C. Rivers, portrayed by Rich Smith, gets in a "cat fight" with a Bobcat during the September 24 game with Jones Junior College.

Wildcats
take the win
against Perk

Terry Carter (5) gets tackled as he attempts to catch the ball during the October 1 game with the Gulf Coast Community College Bulldogs which the Wildcats won 21-14.

Eric Brister, left, carries the ball up the field during the third quarter.

Chris Watts tackles a Perk player while Blaine Miller (35) looks on.

Wildcats take Homecoming Victory

PRC 34   S-W 14

Scooter Byrd, freshman from Purvis, runs up the field with the ball during the October 22 Homecoming game played against Southwest.

Jay Stewart, freshman from Mobile, AL, tackles a "Bear" during the game with the Southwest Bears.

Eric Brister, freshman from Bogalusa, LA, carries the ball up the field to score a touchdown during the Homecoming game.

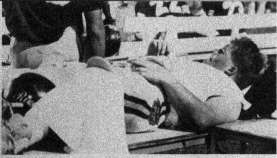

Blaine Miller, freshman from Franklin, LA, watches his fellow teammates roll over the East Central Chiefs 14-0, during the October 15 game.

Frank Denard watches the victory over Coahoma.

Anthony Jurich (36) runs the ball up the field during the third losing game of the season against Co-piah-Lincoln, which the Wildcats lost by ten points, 17-7.

Marvin Keith Smith (39), freshman from Harvey, LA, looks down at his tackled opponent while Anthony Williams (64), freshman from Hattiesburg, looks on during the lost October 8 game with the Northeast Tigers.

Chris Bates, sophomore from Poplarville, tackles a Copiah-Lincoln Wolf while Marvin Keith Smith runs to assist.

Wildcats Go
To Booneville

For Pearl River Community College's participants, the 1988 Mississippi Junior College All-Star game in Booneville could not have been much better, according to PRC head coach Mike Nelson, who, along with his Wildcat staff, guided the South squad to a 24-7 victory over the North.

Nelson said he had a good group of players to work with on the South team, the weather was good and about 55 colleges were represented by scouts at the game.

"And it's always good to win," he added.

This is the second trip to the All-star game for Nelson's staff, which was beaten 10-7 by the North in 1986.

Sophomore running back Roland Johnson, who led the 'Cats with 514 rushing yards during this season, led all rushers in the All-Star game with 84 yards on 12 carries.

On defense, Wildcat linebacker Greg Necaise led both teams with 18 tackles. Necaise was also an All-Region selection.

PRC defensive end Anthony Bowie, wingback Louis Gholar and running back, Tony Jurich also got playing time in the game.

Other Wildcats receiving post season honors included defensive tackle Frank Denard Jr., an All-Region and All-State pick; All-State selection offensive guard Jason Dugas; second team All-State members wide receiver Nolan Booker and defensive back Charles Kindred; and Honorable Mention selections defensive backs Chris Bates and David Johnston.

Nolan Booker made second All-South.

Anthony Bowie made the Mississippi Junior College All-Star team.

Frank Denard Jr. made All-Region and first All-South.

Jason Dugas made first All-South.

Coach Mike Nelson give some helpful pointers to the players.

Coach Nelson discusses some new playing strategies with a player.

Louis Gholar made Mississippi Junior College All-Star team.

Roland Johnson made Mississippi Junior College All-Star team and first All-South.

Anthony Jurich made Mississippi Junior College All-Star team.

Greg Necaise made All-Region, first All-South and Mississippi Junior College All-Star team.

85

Coaches, managers and players alike cele-
brated at the end of the season when the Wildcat
team brought in a 6-3-1 record (above).

William Harper (left) and Louis Gholar enjoy
some sideline fun during a muddy game (right).

Season closes with eleven signed

Four-year colleges and universities looking for football talent didn't leave much behind for others when they got through examining what PRC had to offer in 1988.

Eleven players from the Wildcat football team signed with four-year schools. While the 'Cats had 13 players sign in 1987, 1988's total was proportionally larger. In 1987 there were 34 sophomores on the Wildcat team and in 1988 there were only 14.

The players that were signed were Nolan Booker, a 5-9, 170-pound wide receiver from Covington, who signed with Langston University in Oklahoma. Lewis Gholar, a 6-1, 200-pound wingback from Prentiss, signed with Savannah State in Georgia. Roland Johnson, a 5-11, 214-pound runningback from

Hattiesburg, signed with Troy State. Anthony Jurich, a 5-9, 200-pound runningback from Picayune, signed with Evangel College in Springfield, Mo. Charles Kindred, a 5-10, 170-pound defensive back from Brooklyn, signed with Southern Methodist University. Greg Necaise, a 6-1, 225-pound linebacker from Bay St. Louis signed with Northwestern Louisiana.

Chris Bates, a 6-2, 187-pound defensive back from Poplarville, Anthony Bowie, a 6-2, 230-pound defensive end from Monroe, LA, and David

Johnston, a 5-10, 185-pound defensive back from Picayune have all signed with Oregon Tech.

Brad Greer, a 5-11, 220-pound linebacker from Poplarville, signed with Millsaps College in Jackson. William Earl Harper, a 6-0, 223-pound fullback from Bassfield signed with Langston University.

All these players, no matter how far they go, will be sorely missed by the Coaching staff and players of the Wildcat team.

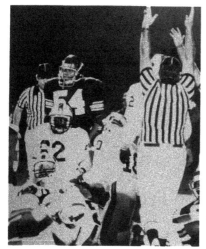

Jackson Hall (54) looks on as a touchdown is signaled by a referee (left).

Sports and sports photography is a messy business as Kevin Ina (51) and Susie Seal will tell anyone. During the season Susie was tackled twice in one game, luckily not injuring her (below).

Taking a break from a rough game, line backer Greg Necaise rests on the bench (above).

Offensive Line Coach Mike Harris gets into the action during preseason workouts (left).

87

Wildcats lacked experience

Overcoming inexperience was the key to the Wildcats' successes this season.

Seven players were gone from last season's squad, which posted a 12-10 record overall and an 8-6 South Division record.

Wendell Carter, a 6-5 forward from Atlanta, GA, was the only returning 'cat with any extensive playing time. Last season Carter averaged 14.3 points and 7.5 rebounds per game.

Also returning, but with less playing time, was Scott Waldrop. Waldrop, a 6-2 guard from Oak Grove held one of the starting positions.

Among the players joining the Wildcat team was Andrew Neely. The 6-8 center from Atlanta, GA, was one of the teams key players due to his height.

Raymond Nash, a 6-6 freshman from St. Amant, LA, played at the forward position, while Horace Washington, a 6-3 freshman from Covington, LA, and Terry Williams, a 6-4 Freshman from Picayune shared time at the guard spot opposite Waldrop.

In addition, Micheal Boutee, a 5-9 freshman from Church Point, LA, Rico Foxworth, a 6-1 freshman from Columbia, and Charles Kindred, a 5-11 sophomore from Brooklyn, saw time at the guard spots.

Despite the lack of maturity, however, coach Peter Georgian said he was excited about the season.

"I think if we gain enough experience we can push for a Division title," said Georgian, adding that this year's team has plenty of depth and good attitude.

In the past two seasons since he has been here, Georgian said the team has had six to seven people who could play. This year he will have as many as nine who could hold their own as starters.

He also said the team had worked hard in the preseason to get 88 ready for the year.

Charzis Silas, of Hattiesburg, goes for the hoop while an opponent tries to block her.

Wildcat Head Coach Peter Georgian and Student Coach Marty Noblitt discuss playing strategies while the players look on.

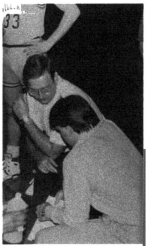

Lady 'Cats Aim for the Top

The 1988-89 Lady Wildcats started the season off with high hopes. These high hopes were affirmed by the 20-9 record of the 1987 season.

Among the players returning to the Lady 'Cat team was the 6-2 center from Picayune, Antrice McGill. Last season McGill averaged 22.2 points and 7.8 rebounds for Pearl River Community College and was named to the All-State and All-Region teams.

Mary "Cocoa" Henry, a 5-6 guard from Poplarville, was another returning player. During last season she averaged 12 points and almost six rebounds per game.

Mary Arvel, a 5-6 guard from Donaldsonville, LA, was a reserve player for the team last year, but got a good bit of playing time.

Suzanne Smith, a 5-6 guard from Oak Grove, also returned to the Wildcat team.

In addition to the returning players Lady Wildcat Head Coach Polly Kirkland said that she had some fine young freshmen coming in to fill the gaps left by last year's sophomores.

Edith Pedecleaux, a 5-11 forward from Donaldsonville, and Charzis Silas, a 5-11 forward from Hattiesburg, were freshman starters for the team.

The extra help and the over-all team experience came in handy against what Kirkland called a much tougher schedule.

"This year we've tried purposely to toughen up the schedule," said Kirkland. "To be the best, you've got to play the best."

She said against this schedule her team which averaged almost 78 points per game last year, would have to play stingier defense.

On offense, she said, the Lady Wildcats will try to use their good team height to their advantage on the inside.

"We will be taking the ball inside a lot," Kirkland said. "We will break when we can, but we won't just run and gun. If we don't out-number them we'll slow it up and set up our offense."

Andrew Neely, of Atlanta, GA, puts one in while opposing players crowd the 6-8 freshman.

89

Men's Basketball

Wildcats

Wendell Carter was knocked down during a game with the Jones County Junior College Bobcats (above). After the incident occurred Wendell and the other player discussed it with the referee.

Mark Stringer goes for the ball while an opposing player blocks him.

Wendell Carter makes an appeal to the referee while a freethrow is being made (below).

Larry Acker gets the ball taken away, by an opposing player, as he goes for the layup (below left).

Wildcats

Above are the members of the 1988-'89 Wildcat Basketball team. Kneeling from left are Larry Acker, of Bay St. Louis; Alonzo Ward, of Brooklyn; Mark Stringer, of West Marion; Micheal Boutee, of Church Point, La. Standing are Horace Washington, of Covington La.; Antonio Berry, of Hattiesburg; Andrew Neely, of Atlanta, Ga.; Wendell Carter, of Atlanta, Ga.; and Terry Williams, of Picayune.

Wildcat Head Coach Peter Georgian

Wildcat Student Coach Marty Noblitt

The 1988-'89 Wildcat Managers are Cortez Vaughn and Kenny Byers. (not pictured is Scott Nease)

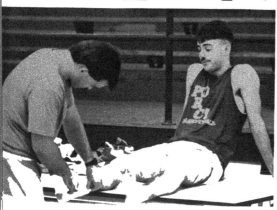

Micheal Boute, of Church Point, LA. lays one up during the game with Natchez Community College.

Scott Waldrop gets his ankle taped during a practice session.

Andrew Neely scores during the first game of the season.

Mark Stringer (left) blocks an opposing player (above).

Alonzo Ward goes for a layup (above right).

Mark Stringer along with other players watch the Wildcats roll one over (right).

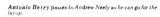

Antonio Berry passes to Andrew Neely so he can go for the layup.

Wendell Carter goes for the layup. (below left)

Michael Boutee throws one in. (below)

Raymond Nash dribbles to the goal while an opposing team member follows closely. (below right)

(Photos by James Stewart)

95

Women's Basketball

Lady Wildcats

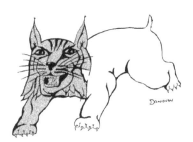

Mary Arvel carries the ball up the court during the game with the Jefferson Davis War Hawks.

Katrina Lundy and **Christy Doby** takes stats during a game.

Suzanne Smith goes for the ball while *Antrice McGill* runs to assist.

Coach Kirkland (below left) gives playing instructions during the game.

Charzes Silas (below) reaches for the rebound.

(Photos by James Stewart)

The Lady Wildcats

Above are the members of the 1988-'89 Lady Wildcat Basketball team. They are, kneeling from left, Mary Henery, of Poplarville; Cami Cox, of Columbia; Mary Arvel, of Donaldsonville, LA; Suzanne Smith, of Oak Grove; Sharon Maxwell, of Brooklyn. Standing from left, are Gwen Stringer, of Prentiss; Jori Barnett, of Lafayette, LA; Antrice McGill, of Picayune; Edith Pedescleaux, of Donaldsonville, LA; Charzes Silas, of Hattiesburg; and Natalie Ladner, of Pass Christian.

Lady Wildcat Head Coach Polly Kirkland

Lady Wildcat Assistant Coach Lesia Duncan

Lady Wildcat Managers are, from left, Gina Stringer, Antha Dupont, Satoy Magee and Katrina Lundy.

Antrice McGill (33) shoots a basket during the game with Holmes Junior College where she broke her own scoring record of 43 points in a game, by scoring 46 points. *Edith Pedecleaux* (31) looks on with hope that the ball goes in.

Suzanne Smith looks for an open man on the Wildcat Court. *Gwen Stringer* shoots a basket while W.C. Rivers looks on.

A Hinds player steals the rebound from Antrice McGill.

Mary Arvel (above left) passes to Charzis Silas during a heated game.

Coach Polly Kirkland gives some orders during a time-out.

(Photos by James Stewart)

Antrice McGill makes a layup.

Natalie Ladner *(12) blocks an opposing player during the game (below left).*

Natalie Ladner *signals to another player that she is open for a pass (below).*

Coach Lesia Duncan *and Sharon Maxwell enjoy a relaxing moment on the bench (below left).*

Coaches have similar views on seasons

Though their records were much different, the coaches for both Pearl River Community College's basketball team's had much the same feelings about their season's outcomes.

Both were disappointed their records did not turn out better, but they were pleased with the performance of their players.

For the Lady Wildcats, who posted a 15-12 record, the season did not end nearly as well as expected. The squad was picked as one of the top teams in the state by pre-season polls, but was eliminated from post season play by East Central 95-77 in the first frame of the South Division Tournament.

Peter Georgian, coach of the men's team, knew that his squad faced a tough year with only two players returning from last season, but things were even worse, with discipline problems and injuries playing havoc with the roster, and leaving the 'Cats with only six players on the team at the end of the year, which endowed with a 95-54 loss to Southwest, leaving them with a 6-23 record overall and 1-11 mark in the division.

But Georgian said those numbers tell little of the story.

He said he was pleased with the efforts of those players who stuck it out, expecially walk-ons Larry Acker and Mark Stringer, who were able to contribute to the team more than expected.

"I don't see their dedication, effort and attitude to play with others for the good of the team reflected in our record," Georgian said. "I also don't see their sweat and personal victories."

"The six guys we ended up with in the playoffs at Perkington were all dedicated, unselfish, and devoted to Pearl River Community College and our team," he said. "This is the record I carry away from the season."

Polly Kirkland, coach of the women's team, said little could have been done to change the outcome of her squad's early loss.

East Central shot 80 percent from the floor in the game.

"When somebody's that hot, it's tough to win," Kirkland said.

When they make them falling down, there's not much you can do about it," she said of the Lady Warriors' ability to sink shots even when being fouled.

She said she was happy with the team's effort in the game, however.

Antrice McGill, the team's leading scorer, was able to score 26 points and pull down 10 rebounds despite being hampered by torn ligaments in her right ankle.

Antrice McGill shoots a hoop during the South Division tournament at Perkingston. Horace Washington (left) passes to the inside man at the Perkingston tournament.

Horace Washington carries the ball to the goal during the South Division tournament.

Wendell Carter - South All-Stars team and second team All-State

Antrice McGill - All-State, All-South team

Raymond Nash - Honorable Mention - All-State

Andrew Neely - Second Team All-State

Charsiz Silas - All-Region

Alonzo Ward - Honorable Mention All-State

Wildcats' Results

Our Score	Opp.	Opp. Score
74	Natchez	77
77	Meridian	66
73	Natchez	82
83	Jeff Davis	73
54	Holmes	81
86	Hinds	93
65	Pensacola, Fla.	91
67	Trinity Valley, Tex.	87
91	L.B. Wallace, Ala.	77
98	East Central	94
91	Delgado, La.	108
96	Natchez	86
65	Bossier	69
64	Co-Lin	75
60	Southwest	73
97	Delgado	101
63	Holmes	68
90	Jeff Davis, Ala.	74
77	Hinds	82
56	Gulf Coast	76
78	Jones	88
73	East Central	73
65	Natchez	80
56	Co-Lin	115
63	Southwest	86
51	Hinds	70
56	Gulf Coast	79
74	Jones	107
54	Southwest	95

Lady 'Cats' Results

Our Score	Opp.	Opp. Score
81	Cleveland State, Tenn.	53
68	Pensacola, Fla.	72
82	Patrick Henry, Ala.	76
72	Clarke College	68
87	Jeff Davis, Ala.	59
80	Jeff Davis, Ala.	53
78	Itawamba	97
84	East Central	86
78	Trinity Valley, Tex.	80
70	Panola Jr. College, Tex.	90
49	Co-Lin	57
92	Southwest	76
79	Holmes	69
69	Jeff Davis, Ala.	103
72	Hinds	90
78	Gulf Coast	87
91	East Central	65
86	Pensacola, Fla.	64
54	Co-Lin	58
69	Southwest	62
71	Clarke	69
59	Hinds	68
80	Gulf Coast	72
80	Pensacola	54
79	Jones	56
77	East Central	95

103

Wildcat Baseball Coach Jim Nightengale

Wildcats start season strong

Last Season the Pearl River Community College baseball team made a pretty good showing, and head coach Jim Nightengale said the ingredients were there for the Wildcats to do even better during his second year at the helm.

In 1988 the Wildcats put together a 25-13 record, going all the way to the Region 23 tournament, and this year the line-up included as many as seven starters from that group.

"That's why I feel a little more confident in the close ball games," Nightengale said.

While having experienced players is always important, Nightengale said it is especially important in the community college ranks.

"The first year they are trying to feel their way through it," he said, pointing out that for many players it is their first time away from home, and they are having to adjust to a new baseball program.

But the experience of going to the playoffs last season gave the 'Cats an added boost this spring. "I'm hoping that among those returning this season was Jay Artigues of Bay St. Louis, who started at second base. As a freshman Artigues led the team with a .414 average and 18 stolen bases.

Nightengale said that Artiguez' team-leading 37 walks last season is another indication of his importance to the squad's offense, which was a powerful weapon.

As a team the 'Cats hit .342 and scored 342 runs.

Mike Weems of Bay St. Louis provided the power of his catching abilities. Last season Weems was tied for the team lead with six homeruns and was second in RBIs with 31.

"We've got some people who can swing the bat," Nightengale said. Last season the 'Cats had trouble putting opponents away in the late innings.

This spring he counted on Bobby Jackson of Old Town, Minn. and Jesse Logan of Bay St. Louis to be his stoppers.

He added that Jackson was probably his best all-around, capable of playing almost any defensive position. He also hit .346 last season.

The addition of Jimmy Agent, an all-state player from Oak Grove, and Todd Bergeron, an all-district player from Central High School of Baton Rouge.

On defense, Brian Laneaux of Bay St. Louis and Ty Henery of Baton Rouge shared time at first base, Jimmy Miller of Purvis shared time at third with Jackson.

Freshman Martin Poche of Baton Rouge started at shortstop to round out the infield.

When not pitching, Jesse Logan helped Devan Mohr, of Hattiesburg, with duties in right field. Ben Jones of Gary, Ind. was the starter in center field, and Paul Powell of Petal, a .320 hitter last year, started in left field.

Todd Bergeron mows the grass at the Wildcat Diamond.

Fall Baseball

Catcher Mike Weems of Bay St. Louis tries to catch a runner on his way to second.

Jay Artigues follows through on his swing.

Outfielder Paul Powell of Petal (left) gets a high-five.

Paul Powell dives back to first to avoid the tag.

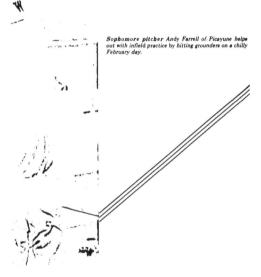

Sophomore pitcher Andy Farrell of Picayune helps out with infield practice by hitting grounders on a chilly February day.

Practice

Ty Henry (top right) gets ready to backhand the ball at first, while Jimmy Miller (left) eyes a chopper at third and shortstop Martin Poche (above) follows through on his throw to home.

B *P*
a *r*
t *a*
t *c*
i *t*
n *i*
####### *g* *c*
######## *e*

Jay Artigues (above) fights off an inside pitch, while Bobby Jackson, pitcher/third baseman from Old Town, Minn., sharpens his swing using a batting-t.

Jesse Logan, pitcher/outfielder from Bay St. Louis, waits for a pitch from the pitching machine.

Grant Kohnke feeds a ball to the pitching machine.

y Henry works out on the batting-t.

Intramurals

Pictured below are the Skulls, winners of the Intramural Flag Football Championship. Kneeling from left are Britt Wood, Irvin Templett, Crisper Stanford, and Geza Carter. Standing are Mark Necaise, Aurthur Wynne, Mike Haverdy, Kevin Ladner, Gregg Foster, and Mark Haverty.

Pictured above are the winners of the 1988 Bloomer Bowl, the sophomores. Kneeling from left are Traci Selman, Susie Seal, Jennifer Hyatt, Angela Smith and Jill Dodd. Standing are Coach Joey Spino, Jan Holeman, Lynn Seal, Angela Haddox, Coach Greg Necaise, Captain Tracey Cook, Taren Breland, and Coach Crisper Stanford.

Angela Haddox gets a helping hand from Jennifer Hyatt during the Bloomer Bowl.

112

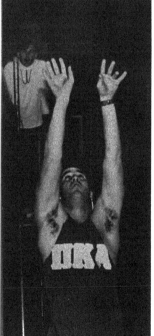

Above are the members of the Sly Dogs, the winners of the 1988 Intramural Volleyball Championships. Kneeling from left are Britt Wood, Kyle Ward, Mark Haverty. Standing are Kevin Ladner, Danny Mannely, and Geza Carter.

To the left is Britt Wood reaching for the ball as Jan Fletcher, referee, looks on.

Above left are the members of the Better Halves, winners of the 1988 Intramural Co-Rec Volleyball Championships. Kneeling are Darlene Minton, Anita Mosely, Dotsie Nussbaum, and Missy Greater. Standing are Captain Daniel Dorion, Brad Malone, Mitch Biancato, and Chuck Babiowski.

Lou Thomas, of the Misfits, and Daniel Dorion of the Better Halves battle it out during the championship.

Intramurals

Checkers
Ping-Pong Singles
Pong-Ping Doubles
Mens 8-ball
Womens 8-ball

Robert Hicks *(above), a cabinet making major from Prentiss, won the 1988 Intramural Checkers Championship.*

Lonnie Vaughn *(above right), a electrical major from Carriere, won the 1988 Intramural Ping-Pong Singles Championship.*

Travis Kennedy, *an Electronic Engineering major from Carriere, and Randy Sanford, an Electronics major from Carriere, won the Intramural Ping Pong Doubles Championship (right).*

Russell Lee *(right), a Drafting and Design major from Picayune, won the Intramural 8-ball Mens Championship.*

Melissa Greater *(Far right), a sophomore from Poplarville, won the Intramural 8-ball Womens Championship.*

Spades

Marty Pullman plays in the winning game of spades.

Brian Ezell, a psychology major from Purvis, and Marty Pullman, a psychology major from Petal, won the Intramural Spades Championship.

Pearl River College's

Former Athletes Honored

The 1988 Pearl River Community College Homecoming will be remembered for several things - among those will be the induction of the first Pearl River College Hall of Fame members.

The eight charter members of the newly-formed PRC Sports Hall of Fame were inducted at the October 22 homecoming game.

The inductees were former PRC coaches Edwin "Goat" Hale and T.D. "Dobie" Holden, 1926 quarterback Jack Read of Picayune, 1948-'49 quarterback Frank Branch of Pascagoula, 1953-'54 tackle Forrest Ball of Columbia, 1955-'57 basketball star Larry Ladner of Hattiesburg, 1969-'70 running back Willie Heidleburg of Jackson and 1976-'78 Lady Wildcat Basketball player Toni Byrd of Bay St. Louis.

After the halftime performance by the Spirit of the River, Donna Wilson, director of the Development Foundation/Alumni Affairs Office, and Dr. John Grant, physic instructor at PRC, inducted eight charter members into PRC's first Sports Hall of Fame.

In order to become a member of the Hall of Fame a person must be voted in unanimously by the Hall of Fame Committee.

Toni Byrd was happy she was picked, saying, "It's a great honor." Byrd added, "I guess someone thought enough of my abilities while I was here and wanted to recognize women's sports, so they picked me."

The oldest living member of the Hall of Fame is Jack Read of Picayune. Read was also recognized as the oldest alumni at the alumni luncheon.

"It's quite an honor to be selected for something for the first time," said Read. He added, "I was really surprised when I was told that I had been selected." While Read was quarterback at PRC, he led the Wildcats to a 6-1 mark.

The newest football star to be included in the Hall of Fame was Willie Heidelburg, now a teacher at Jackson Murrah High School. Heidelburg holds the record for the most yards gained in a season, at PRC, at 910.

"I don't know why I was selected but it's quite an honor," said Heidelburg at the homecoming induction ceremonies.

Shown above are the members or their representatives of the newly-formed PRC Sports Hall of Fame.

Forrest Ball, at PRC 1955-'57.

Frank Branch, at PRC 1948-'49.

Toni Byrd, at PRC 1976-'78.

Sports Hall of Fame

Edwin "Goat" Hale, at PRC 1922-'26, 1936.

Willie Heidelburg, at PRC 1969-'70.

Willie Heidelberg receives his Hall of Fame plaque from Joe Hutchins at the induction ceremonies.

T.D. "Dobie" Holden, at PRC 1948-'66.

Larry Ladner, at PRC 1955-'57.

Jack Read, at PRC 1926.

117

Treasures

of the

River

Faculty, Staff and Administration

Pate Lumpkin
Secretary - Pearl River County

Terrell Randolph
Hancock County

Emil Pav, Jr.
Lamar County

Pearl River
County

Jack Stewart
Board Member
1978-1988

Jackanell Smith
1989

Pearl River's President

Dr. Ted J. Alexander

Ted J. Alexander was named the ninth president of Pearl River Community College by the institution's Board of Trustees and assumed office July 1, 1986.

Dr. Alexander had been Superintendent of Schools for the McComb Municipal Separate District for 10 years before coming to PRC.

He received a B.A. degree from Millsaps College and Master of Education degrees in Education Administration and Guidance from Mississippi College and a Doctor of Education degree from the University of Southern Mississippi. His professional memberships include the American Association of Community and Junior Colleges, the Mississippi Association of School Administrators, and the American Association of School Administrators, the Association for the Supervision and Curriculum Development, the American Association of School Personnel Administrators, and he is a member of the honorary fraternity Phi Delta Kappa. He is also a recipient of the Outstanding School Administrator Award presented by the Mississippi Alliance for Arts Education, a Phil Hardin Scholar and the recipient of a doctorial studies scholarship from the Phil Hardin Foundation. He was also named as a member of the Omni International Omni Publications National Panel of Experts in the 1985-86 school year. He served as Mississippi's lay delegate to the White House Conference on Library and Information Services, and in January, 1987, was designated by the Executive Educator and the American School Board Journal's independent panel of jurors as one of North America's top 100 school executives. He also serves as chair of the Mississippi Humanities Council.

Dr. Alexander addresses faculty in an orientation meeting.

Alexander makes point at a meeting

131

Ron Holmes
Business Manager

Dr. Miller Hammill
Dean of Student Affairs

Dr. Willis Lott
Dean of Academic Affairs

Dr. James Sones
Dean of
Vocational-Technical
Affairs

Administration

Dr. Rebecca Askew
Guidance, Recruitment
and Orientation Director

Mark Bounds
Industrial Training
Coordinator

Mike Dobbins
Financial Aid Director
Spring

Jennifer Downey
Director of Research
Administration, Grants
Proposal Development

Administration

Dow Ford
Admissions Director

Vernetta Fairley
Financial Aid Director
Fall

Charlotte Odom
Director of Nursing

Harvey Seligman
Director of Student Activities

Administration

Donna Wilson
Development Foundation and Alumni
Affairs Director

Don Welsh
Vocational-Technical Director

Martha Brooks Brown
Single Parent/Displaced Homemakers Department

Dr. O.C. Dauenhauer
Academics

134

Counselors

Melissa Smith
Vocational-Technical

Ann Moore
Vocational-Technical

Pearl River Faculty and Staff

Kenneth Adams
Machine Shop
Elizabeth Alsworth
History
Pat Amacker
Cosmetology
Susan Anderson
Computer Technology

Kay Ard
Book Store
Mack Avery
Related Math
James Barnes
Chemistry
Karen Barron
Loan Clerk

Ethel Batson
Remedial Reading
Kathleen Bogle
Math
Beverly Boone
Marketing
Grace Boone
Book Store Manager

Peggy Broomhall
Nursing
Joan Brown
Secretary
Mary Brumfield
Math
Elden Buel
Electronics

Linda Buffington
Nursing
Julia Carson
English
Gail Catoire
Secretary
Peggy Ciccarelli
Reading

Henry Conerly
Biology
Nancy Cook
Financial Aid
Rebecca Dale
Nursing
Phyllis Daniels
Business Technology

Pearl River Faculty and Staff

Shirley Daniels
Financial Aid Secretary
Anne Dauenhauer
Librarian
Jessie Davis
Welding
Regina Davenport
Business Law

Peggy Dease
Nursing
Valerie DeCoux
Nursing
Ann Donnell
Nursing
Susan Donohue
History

Sybil Downes
Nursing
Kim DuBoise
Art
Ann Dugan
Nursing
Jeanne Dyar
Head Librarian

James Elbers
Electricity
Celly Farmer
Barbering
Charles Ferguson
Biology
Ina Flynt
Head Resident

Eddy Gammel
Drafting
Beren Gaule
English
Peter Georgian
History and Physical
Education
John Grant
Physics

Norma Hammill
Biology
Gerald Hampton
Chemistry
Danny Harris
Drafting
Lavonne Henley
Accounting

Pearl River Faculty and Staff

Sarah Henry
Records Clerk
Terry Herndon
Electrician
Carl Hicks
Diesel Mechanics
Libby High
Nursing

Thomas Hill
Auto Mechanics
Bruce Hoem
English
Jean Hoem
Psychology
Jack Holland
Diesel Mechanics

Connie Holmes
Speech, Theatre
Judy Holston
Secretary
Edith Hoover
Head Resident
Steve Howard
Computer Science

Major Hudson
Welding
Roy Jones
Auto Mechanics
Dorothy Jordan
Librarian
Elaine Kersh
Nursing

Polly Kirkland
Math
Bill Kirkpatrick
Philosophy
Michael Knippers
Speech
James Lee
Air-Conditioning

Madelyn Lee
Music
Mark Lott
Carpentry
Rose Lott
Accounts Payable Clerk
Lindsay Loustalot
Nursing

Pearl River Faculty and Staff

Walter Lowe
Social Studies
Mark Malone
Music
Bonnie McCaskell
Nursing
Kathryn Meighen
Head Resident

Donette Mensah
Economics
Catherine Merrikin
Business Technology
Ann Morris
Business Technology
Roese Neves
Electronics

Charlotte Odom
Nursing
Sara Patten
English
Walter Peckham
Machine Shop
Mary Peddicord
English

Wyndal Peterson
Computer Technology
Virginia Pitts
Remedial Math
Margaret Pollock
Secretary
Janice Poole
Secretary

Archie Rawls
Band
Stacy Reese
Computer Operator
Jack Regan
Drafting
Nancy Regan
Business Technology

Charles Reeter
Masonry
Judy Roane
Math
Carolyn Ruegger
Math
Donna Rushton
Nursing

Pearl River Faculty and Staff

Linda Siebenkittel
Business Technology
Phyllis Simoneaux
Accounts Record Clerk

Dolores Smith
Business Education
Celicia Senes
Nurse
Willie Speights
Head Resident

James Stewart
Journalism
Shirley Stockman
Payroll Clerk
Pat Strahan
Records Clerk
Thomas Strebeck
English

DeAnne Terrell
Psychology
Nancy Torre
Nursing
Krista Wade
Accounts Receivable
Clerk
David Whisnant
Cafeteria Manager

Jane Whorton
English
Diana Williams
Nursing
Brenda Windham
Business Technology

Barbara Wise
Secretary
James Young
Electronics
Frances Rawls
Bookstore

Forrest County Vo-Tech Center

Cecil Burt
Director

Jack Batte
Counselor

Joe Wesley
Counselor

Tommy Batte
Masonry
Susan Bedwell
Nurses Aid
Andrew Blackwell
Electronics
Dwayne Desoto
Automotive

Kirk Drennen
Electronics
Nancy Easterling
Nursing
Edwin Elkins
Diversified Technology
JoAnn Eure
Business Education

Clifton Evans, Sr.
Respiratory Therapy
Louis Fairly
Carpentry
Debbie Fendley
Nursing
Dwight Green
Welding

Audrey Hammond
Basic Education
Kathy Hogan
Respiratory Therapy
Len Landrum
Metal Trades
Janes Lewis
Micro-Computer
Specialist

141

Forrest County Vo-Tech Center

Sue Meador
Operating Room Technology
James Robbins
Automotive Mechanics
Linda Smith
Nursing

Hancock County Vo-Tech Center

Alvin Bourgeois
Director

Woody Pearce
Counselor

Doris Allen
Nursing
John Cranmer
Welding
Daryl Ladner
Drafting
Reggie Ladner
Metal Trades

C. H. Miley
Building Trades
Al Saucier
Automotive Mechanics
James Wolf
Electricity
Darnell Cuevas
Business Education

142

Lamar County Vo-Tech Center

Bruce Hankins
Director

John Geraci
Counselor

Billy Blackwell
Auto Mechanics
Judy Britt
Business Education

Tommy Carney
Drafting
Thomas Johnston
Metal Trades

Martha Morris
Nursing
William Salter
Building Trade

Yvonne Wilson
Sales and Marketing

These very busy and efficient secretaries took a precious moment to have their picture taken. Above is Diana Whisnant of Dr. Lott's office. Upper right is Janis Williams, who works for PRCC President, Dr. Ted Alexander. Below is (L to R) Tina Simoneaux, Krista Wade, Karen Barron, Shirley Stokeman and Patsy Howard of the Business Office. Right is Gail Catoire and Sarah Malley of the Development Foundation Alumni office.

Top Left, is Rose Lott, accounts payable clerk. *Top Right* is Joan Brown, Secretary to Dr. James Jones. *Bottom Left* is Maria Lewis and Cynthia Hornsby of the Vocational/Technical office. *Bottom Right* is Nancy Cook and Shirley Daniels, both work in the Financial Aid office.

The Cafeteria Staff

Seated left to right: Mary Graham, Jean McDonald, Annie Fowler, Mamie Nixon, David Bowden, David Whisnant, Gloria Bonadonna, Mary Wallace. Standing: LeRoy Nix, Elbert Hart, Olivia Benden, Earnestine Bowden, Murlene Fairley, J.W. Fowlen, Levi Nix, Pauline Seals, Lorena O'Quinn, Lorraine Wiley.

The Grill Staff

Left to right: Joyce Wiley, Annie Travis, Rhonda Byrd, Marilyn Houston, Chip Taylor.

Campus Security

Standing left to right: Troy Smith, Charles Kindja, Lewis Smith, John Robinson.

Amy Bridgers
Research Administration

Julia Ferguson helps a student with an essay.

Chad Pittman pleads his case.

Shawn Walker is absorbed in his Biology project.

Jim Nightengale seems to be lost in thought.

147

Mike Knippers talks to his Speech class.

Martha Brown shows a sweater to a group of students.

Jeanne Dyar waits for the next student who needs some library assistance.

Dr. Chuck Dauenhauer looks for a good article to read.

Coach Harvey Seligman looks on as Jason Hathorn gets some cookies during the February blood drive.

149

Holiday Spirit at The River

Mrs. Barbara Alexander, left, greets Mrs. Kathryn Moody at a reception held for members of the Board of Trustees and other guests.

Walter Cartier (left), Terry Randolph and Macon Holliman joke around at the reception.

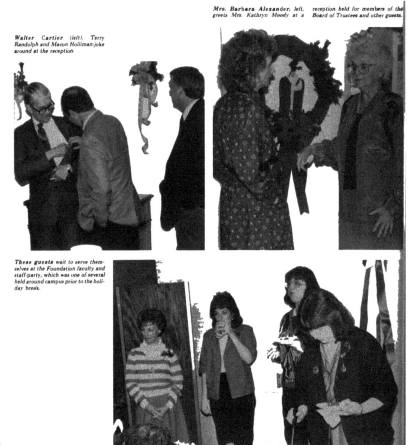

These guests wait to serve themselves at the Foundation faculty and staff party, which was one of several held around campus prior to the holiday break.

Members of the faculty and staff *(above) sample the treats served at the Christmas party hosted by the Development Foundation.*

Ann Morris finds a spot to rest as she enjoys her lunch.

Dr. Mark Malone (below) pours himself a cup of punch.

Dr. Ted Alexander (at right) chats with Thomas Blakeney at an open house at the president's home.

151

Treasures

of the

River

Sophomores

Darlene Acker
Bay St. Louis

Pamela Allen
Poplarville

Mary Arvel
Donaldsonville, LA

Kim Ashe
Poplarville

John Atwood
Lumberton

Doyla Aube
Poplarville

April Austin
Wiggins

Fara Bailey
Lumberton

Bobbie Barber
Columbia

Kristen Barnes
Carriere

Patrick Barnes
Prentiss

Steven Barrett
Purvis

Chris Bates
Poplarville

Rhonda Beall
Lumberton

Kelli Beasley
Hattiesburg

Carolyn Beech
Picayune

Mitch Biancato
Metairie, LA

Betty Bingham
Hattiesburg

Kelli Blackmon
Picayune

Kimberly Bond
Purvis

Steve Bounds
Wiggins

Virginia Bounds
Poplarville

David Bowles
Picayune

154 Darrell Boyd
Carriere

Irene Brady
Sandy Hook

Marilyn Brant
Poplarville

Kim Breakfield
Columbia

Craig Breland
Bay St. Louis

Taren Breland
Pearlington

Virginia Breland
Petal

Alan Bilbo
Columbia

Sophomores

Wanda Breland
Carriere

Colleen Brewer
Picayune

Rhonda Brewer
Morgantown

Donald Brothers
Purvis

Robert Brown
Hattiesburg

Madelyn Bruno
Bay St. Louis

Nancy Byers
Hattiesburg

Matthew Cameron
Bay St. Louis

Geja Cater
Bay St. Louis

Wendell Carter
Poplarville

Debra Chandler
Sumrall

Debbie Clark
Poplarville

Sheri Clunan
Poplarville

Tracey Cook
Hattiesburg

Albert Creel
McNeill

Cindy Cressionnie
McNeill

Darla Daniels
Poplarville

Anna Daughdrill
Poplarville

David Davis
Poplarville

Donna Davis
Poplarville

Jeff Davis
Collins

Michelle Dewease
Slidell, LA

Amanda Dickinson
Hattiesburg

Alice Dillon
Columbia

Jill Dodd
Picayune

Sherman Dodd
Picayune

Daniel Dorion
Bay St. Louis

Jennifer Dossett
Picayune

Cecilia Douglass
Lumberton

Tracy Dupont
Picayune

Sophomores

Candace Emerick
Arabi, LA

Brenda Entrekin
Purvis

Daniel Entrekin
Lumberton

Charmaine Espenschied
Lumberton

Terry Ezell
Purvis

Donald Fail
Picayune

Eric Favre
Bay St. Louis

Suzanne Fendley
Picayune

Julie Ferrill
Poplarville

Catherine Forrest
Bay St. Louis

Sherri Fornea
Columbia

Linda Foster
Picayune

Betty Gardener
Picayune

Donna Gardener
Slidell, LA

Lynn Gaude
Picayune

Patricia Gerald
Richton

Tammy Gibson
Brooklyn

Anita Grimes
Picayune

Paula Guillott
Carriere

Patricia Glass
Picayune

Melissa Graeter
Poplarville

Ed Green
Columbia

Sandra Hall
Bogalusa, LA

156 William Hall
Amite, LA

Ray Hampton
Columbia

Reggie Hanberry
Picayune

Sophomores

Chuck Harrison
Columbia

Mary Henry
Lumberton

Mary J. Henry
Poplarville

Phyllis Henry
Poplarville

Suzanne Hille
Poplarville

Donna Holcomb
Hattiesburg

Pam Hollensbee
Poplarville

Jennifer Hyatt
Carriere

Bobby Jackson
Sandy Hook

Mark Jeanfreau
Picayune

Tammy Jenny
Picayune

Mitch Jones
Columbia

Patricia Kekko
Picayune

Kim Kendrick
Columbia

Ray Kent
Hattiesburg

Chris King
Carriere

Buffy Knight
Perkinston

Kim Koenig
Bay St. Louis

Gidget Ladner
Poplarville

Kevin Ladner
Bay St. Louis

Pamela Ladner
Lumberton

Stephanie Lawless
Bay St. Louis

Jacqueline Lawrence
Columbia

Cindy Lee
McNeill

Kimberly Lee
Brooklyn

Sonya Lee
Poplarville

Sonya Lee
Picayune

Todd Lee
Lumberton

Trudy Lee
Picayune

Melissa Liverett
Bay St. Louis

Jesse Logan
Waveland

Leontyne Lowe
Sumrall

Michael Lowe
Purvis

Katrina Lundy
Purvis

Sophomores

Clayton Magee
Angie, LA

Danny Manley
Carriere

Laura Mars
Picayune

Amanda Martin
Picayune

Mark Masoner
Poplarville

Nancy McBride
Poplarville

Rhonda McCardle
Lumberton

Tanna McCarty
Bogalusa, LA

Kim McClinton
Carriere

Lisa McDonald
Poplarville

Reuben McDowell
Columbia

Antrice McGill
Picayune

Melanie McNabb
Columbia

Dana Meeks
Purvis

Dent Mikell
Prentiss

Elbert Miller
McNeill

Nancy Miller
Sumrall

Teri Miller
Sumrall

Kenny Milligan
Poplarville

Dawn Mitchell
Picayune

Lydia Mitchell
Poplarville

Virginia Morris
Poplarville

Mark Necaise
Bay St. Louis

Michelle Necaise
Picayune

Angela Nelson
Columbia

158 Janice Osby
Bogalusa, LA

Jeff Pace
Sumrall

Dan Page
Columbia

Laretta Page
Hattiesburg

Sophomores

Becky Palmer
Picayune

Charlene Partridge
Slidell, LA

Shannon Patterson
Sumrall

Todd Pearson
Carriere

Dennis Penton
Carriere

Trina Penton
Carriere

Karin Pepiton
Picayune

Tammy Piercy
Hattiesburg

Jennifer Pittman
Columbia

Karen Prewett
Picayune

Sharon Price
Poplarville

Greg Pritchett
Poplarville

Janice Pucheu
Kiln

Marcia Pullen
Lumberton

Marty Pulliam
Petal

Ruth Pulsifer
Kiln

Wesley Putnam
Carriere

Carla Raines
Carriere

Clayton Raine
Poplarville

Kathy Raines
Picayune

Lisa Ramshur
Columbia

Chris Rankin
Lumberton

Leslie Reddick
Poplarville

Wanda Reddick
Poplarville

Tracy Reed
Bay St. Louis

Jon Reid
Poplarville

Linda Reid
Lumberton

Rhonda Reid
Columbia

Larry Reid
Lumberton

Don Regan 159
Columbia

Sophomores

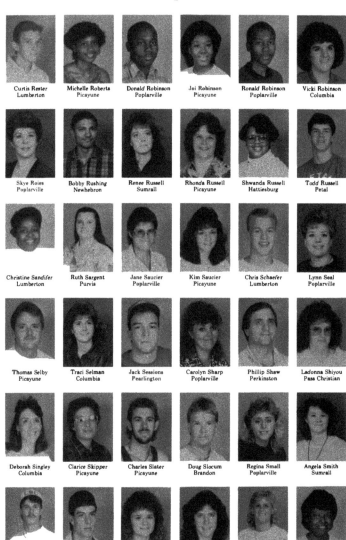

Curtis Rester
Lumberton

Michelle Roberts
Picayune

Donald Robinson
Poplarville

Joi Robinson
Picayune

Ronald Robinson
Poplarville

Vicki Robinson
Columbia

Skye Roies
Poplarville

Bobby Rushing
Newhebron

Renee Russell
Sumrall

Rhonda Russell
Picayune

Shwanda Russell
Hattiesburg

Todd Russell
Petal

Christine Sandifer
Lumberton

Ruth Sargent
Purvis

Jane Saucier
Poplarville

Kim Saucier
Picayune

Chris Schaefer
Lumberton

Lynn Seal
Poplarville

Thomas Selby
Picayune

Traci Selman
Columbia

Jack Sessions
Pearlington

Carolyn Sharp
Poplarville

Phillip Shaw
Perkinston

Ladonna Shiyou
Pass Christian

Deborah Singley
Columbia

Clarice Skipper
Picayune

Charles Slater
Picayune

Doug Slocum
Brandon

Regina Small
Poplarville

Angela Smith
Sumrall

160   Doug Smith
Poplarville

Rafe Smith
Poplarville

Sheila Smith
Poplarville

Sherri Smith
Bay St. Louis

Suzanne Smith
Hattiesburg

Vicki Smith
Picayune

Sophomores

Michael Rogers
Picayune

Rodney Simpson
Picayune

Susie Seal
Picayune

Kathi Short
Poplarville

Donna Smith
Poplarville

Wendi Smith
Carriere

Kirk Stenklyft and Joe Keiter (14) play intramural football.

Jess Spence
Carriere

Alice Spiers
McNeil

Jennifer Spiers
Poplarville

Samantha Stevens
Picayune

Sharon Stewart
Carriere

Below Johnnye Barilleaux, Naomi Barilleaux
and Kim Johnson rest in the shade.

Sophomores

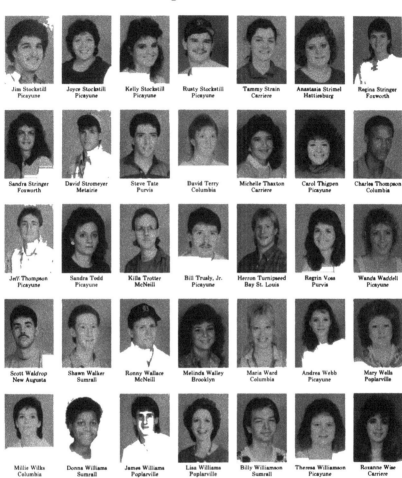

Jim Stockstill
Picayune

Joyce Stockstill
Picayune

Kelly Stockstill
Picayune

Rusty Stockstill
Picayune

Tammy Strain
Carriere

Anastasia Strimel
Hattiesburg

Regina Stringer
Foxworth

Sandra Stringer
Foxworth

David Stromeyer
Metairie

Steve Tate
Purvis

David Terry
Columbia

Michelle Thaxton
Carriere

Carol Thigpen
Picayune

Charles Thompson
Columbia

Jeff Thompson
Picayune

Sandra Todd
Picayune

Killa Trotter
McNeill

Bill Trusly, Jr.
Picayune

Herron Turnipseed
Bay St. Louis

Regrin Voss
Purvis

Wanda Waddell
Picayune

Scott Waldrop
New Augusta

Shawn Walker
Sumrall

Ronny Wallace
McNeill

Melinda Walley
Brooklyn

Maria Ward
Columbia

Andrea Webb
Picayune

Mary Wells
Poplarville

Millie Wilks
Columbia

Donna Williams
Sumrall

James Williams
Poplarville

Lisa Williams
Poplarville

Billy Williamson
Sumrall

Theresa Williamson
Picayune

Roxanne Wise
Carriere

162 William Witsell
Poplarville

Britt Woods
Bay St. Louis

Liz Young
Columbia

Carl Zell, III
Poplarville

Freshmen

Regina Stringer
Foxworth

Charlotte Aborom
Hattiesburg

Ruth Abram
Columbia

Donna Abshire
Slidell, LA

Crystal Acker
Waveland

Furnell Acker
Pearlington

Larry Acker
Pearlington

Donna Adcox
Picayune

Charise Thompson
Columbia

Beth Albritton
Columbia

Vicky Alcalen
Poplarville

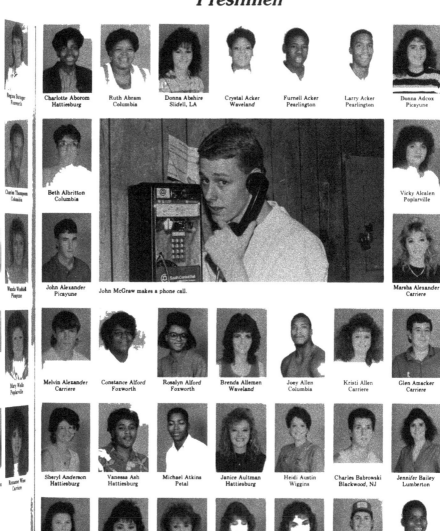

John McGraw makes a phone call.

Wanda Waddell
Picayune

John Alexander
Picayune

Marsha Alexander
Carriere

Mary Wells
Poplarville

Melvin Alexander
Carriere

Constance Alford
Foxworth

Rosalyn Alford
Foxworth

Brenda Allemen
Waveland

Joey Allen
Columbia

Kristi Allen
Carriere

Glen Amacker
Carriere

Roxanne Wise
Carriere

Sheryl Anderson
Hattiesburg

Vanessa Ash
Hattiesburg

Michael Atkins
Petal

Janice Aultman
Hattiesburg

Heidi Austin
Wiggins

Charles Babrowski
Blackwood, NJ

Jennifer Bailey
Lumberton

Sharron Bailey
Foxworth

Angie Barber
Columbia

Tracy Bardwell
Lumberton

Johnnye Barilleaux
Bay St. Louis

Naomi Barilleaux
Bay St. Louis

James Barnes
Poplarville

Jermoine Barnes
Prentiss

Freshmen

Angela Barrett
Lumberton

William Barrett
Lumberton

Harry Barnett, III
Poplarville

Christy Baxter
Picayune

Cassandra Bazor
Perkinston

Connie Beacht
Picayune

Trena Beard
Prentiss

Scott Beith
Carriere

Scott Bello
Pearlington

River Navagators make learning the campus easy.

Charles Bennett
Pearlington

Karen Berger
Lumberton

Antonio Berry
Hattiesburg

Bethany Berry
Sandy Hook

Renee Berry
Prentiss

Cheryl Bethley
Hattiesburg

Rhonda Bilbo
Bay St. Louis

Tommy Bilbo
Carriere

Ray Billeaud, Jr.
Picayune

Rosalyne Blackston
Hattiesburg

DeDe Blackwell
Hattiesburg

Lakeisha Bolton
Poplarville

Ben Bonner
Sumrall

Milton Bourn
Purvis

Tania Breland
Pearlington

Dianna Breshears
Lumberton

Amanda Broom
Poplarville

Charietta Brown
Hattiesburg

Terri Brown
Lumberton

Toby Bryant
Columbia

Randy Burge
Picayune

Ronda Burge
Picayune

Wanda Burkhalter
Lumberton

Freshmen

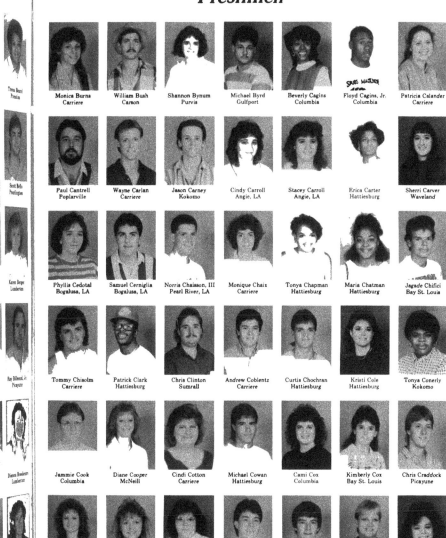

Teresa Beard
Princton

Monica Burns
Carriere

William Bush
Carson

Shannon Bynum
Purvis

Michael Byrd
Gulfport

Beverly Cagins
Columbia

Floyd Cagins, Jr.
Columbia

Patricia Calander
Carriere

Scott Bells
Pentlington

Paul Cantrell
Poplarville

Wayne Carlan
Carriere

Jason Carney
Kokomo

Cindy Carroll
Angie, LA

Stacey Carroll
Angie, LA

Erica Carter
Hattiesburg

Sherri Carver
Waveland

Karen Berger
Lumberton

Phyllis Cedotal
Bogalusa, LA

Samuel Cerniglia
Bogalusa, LA

Norris Chaisson, III
Pearl River, LA

Monique Chaix
Carriere

Tonya Chapman
Hattiesburg

Maria Chatman
Hattiesburg

Jagade Chifici
Bay St. Louis

Ray Billeaud, Jr.
Picayune

Tommy Chisolm
Carriere

Patrick Clark
Hattiesburg

Chris Clinton
Sumrall

Andrew Coblentz
Carriere

Curtis Chochran
Hattiesburg

Kristi Cole
Hattiesburg

Tonya Conerly
Kokomo

Dianna Bonderen
Lumberton

Jammie Cook
Columbia

Diane Cooper
McNeill

Cindi Cotton
Carriere

Michael Cowan
Hattiesburg

Cami Cox
Columbia

Kimberly Cox
Bay St. Louis

Chris Craddock
Picayune

Wanda Burkhalter
Lumberton

Teresa Craft
Picayune

Tiffanie Craft
Picayune

Deborah Crouchet
Picayune

Anthony Cuevas
Poplarville

Charles Culpepper
Poplarville

Andra Cutrer
Picayune

Deborah Daley
Carson

165

Freshmen

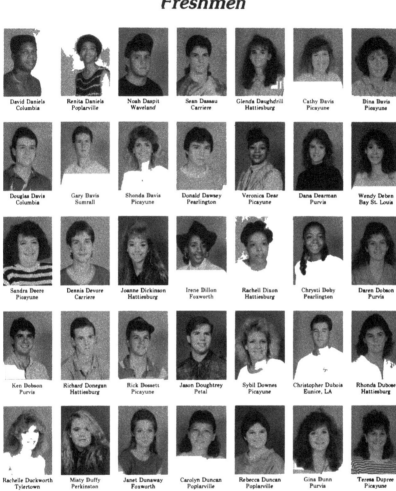

David Daniels
Columbia

Renita Daniels
Poplarville

Noah Daspit
Waveland

Sean Dassau
Carriere

Glenda Daughdrill
Hattiesburg

Cathy Davis
Picayune

Dina Davis
Picayune

Douglas Davis
Columbia

Gary Davis
Sumrall

Shonda Davis
Picayune

Donald Dawsey
Pearlington

Veronica Dear
Picayune

Dana Dearman
Purvis

Wendy Deben
Bay St. Louis

Sandra Deere
Picayune

Dennis Devore
Carriere

Joanne Dickinson
Hattiesburg

Irene Dillon
Foxworth

Rachell Dixon
Hattiesburg

Chrysti Doby
Pearlington

Daren Dobson
Purvis

Ken Dobson
Purvis

Richard Donegan
Hattiesburg

Rick Dossett
Picayune

Jason Doughtrey
Petal

Sybil Downes
Picayune

Christopher Dubois
Eunice, LA

Rhonda Dubose
Hattiesburg

Rachelle Duckworth
Tylertown

Misty Duffy
Perkinston

Janet Dunaway
Foxworth

Carolyn Duncan
Poplarville

Rebecca Duncan
Poplarville

Gina Dunn
Purvis

Teresa Dupree
Picayune

166 Cindy Dyess
Columbia

Donna Edmunds
Poplarville

John Edwards
Columbia

Lisa Entrekin
Carriere

Lisa Eure
Hattiesburg

Lindsey Evans
Hattiesburg

Jennifer Perrill
Poplarville

Freshmen

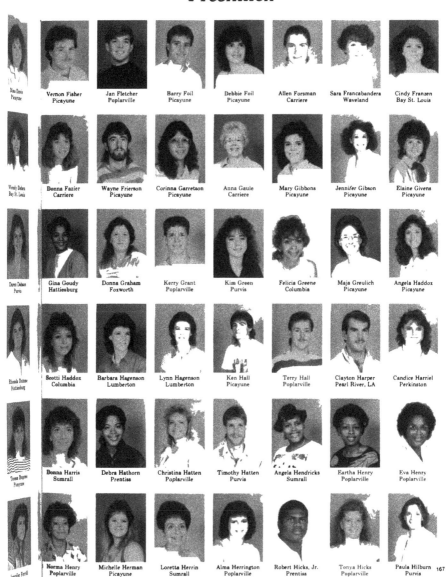

Dian Davis
Picayune

Vernon Fisher
Picayune

Jan Fletcher
Poplarville

Barry Foil
Picayune

Debbie Foil
Picayune

Allen Forsman
Carriere

Sara Francabandera
Waveland

Cindy Franzen
Bay St. Louis

Wendy Dulan
Bay St. Louis

Donna Fazier
Carriere

Wayne Frierson
Picayune

Corinna Garretson
Picayune

Anna Gaule
Carriere

Mary Gibbons
Picayune

Jennifer Gibson
Picayune

Elaine Givens
Picayune

Davee Dobson
Purvis

Gina Goudy
Hattiesburg

Donna Graham
Foxworth

Kerry Grant
Poplarville

Kim Green
Purvis

Felicia Greene
Columbia

Maja Greulich
Picayune

Angela Haddox
Picayune

Rhonda Dubose
Hattiesburg

Scotti Haddox
Columbia

Barbara Hagenson
Lumberton

Lynn Hagenson
Lumberton

Ken Hall
Picayune

Terry Hall
Poplarville

Clayton Harper
Pearl River, LA

Candice Harriel
Perkinston

Teresa Dupree
Picayune

Donna Harris
Sumrall

Debra Hathorn
Prentiss

Christina Hatten
Poplarville

Timothy Hatten
Purvis

Angela Hendricks
Sumrall

Eartha Henry
Poplarville

Eva Henry
Poplarville

Jennifer Ferril
Poplarville

Norma Henry
Poplarville

Michelle Herman
Picayune

Loretta Herrin
Sumrall

Alma Herrington
Poplarville

Robert Hicks, Jr.
Prentiss

Tonya Hicks
Poplarville

Paula Hilburn
Purvis

167

Freshmen

Darold Hill
Atlanta, GA

Lisa Hinton
Hattiesburg

Kim Bond and Ruth Pulsifer obviously enjoy Pep Band.

Linda Hollander
Poplarville

Tracy Honeycutt
Columbia

Bradley Honomich
Hattiesburg

Sabrina Hooker
Hattiesburg

Tammy Howard
Poplarville

Clint Hudson
Hattiesburg

Lisa Hughes
Columbia

April Humphrey
Poplarville

Cathy Hunt
Poplarville

Bryan Jackson
Bassfield

Lora Johnson
Columbia

Monice Johnson
Columbia

Stacey Johnson
Petal

Victoria Johnson
Hattiesburg

Teresa Jones
Poplarville

Teresa Keef
Picayune

Brad Keith
Purvis

Greg Kellar
Picayune

Luwanda Kellar
Picayune

Thomas Kendrick
Columbia

Marrell Marsh
Lumberton

Deborah
Pet

Jerry Kihlken
Picayune

Brian Kimball
Poplarville

Ira Knight
Columbia

Susan Knue
Lumberton

Sharon Koenenn
Kiln

Angie Ladner
Lumberton

Craig Ladner
Perkinston

Regina McCall
Picayune

Prentl
C

Jason Ladner
Columbia

Leslie Ladner
Bay St. Louis

Mary Ladner
Hattiesburg

Natalie Ladner
Pass Christian

Rhonda Ladner
Poplarville

Rhett Ladner
Pass Christian

Robbie Ladner
Poplarville

Lorena McKean
Carriere

Pass
Ne

Jami

Melis

Freshmen

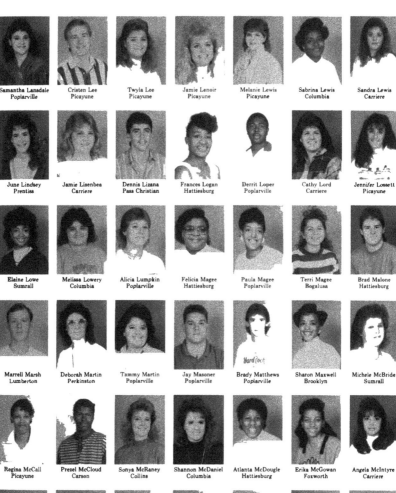

Samantha Lansdale Poplarville	Cristen Lee Picayune	Twyla Lee Picayune	Jamie Lenoir Picayune	Melanie Lewis Picayune	Sabrina Lewis Columbia	Sandra Lewis Carriere
June Lindsey Prentiss	Jamie Lisenbea Carriere	Dennis Lizana Pass Christian	Frances Logan Hattiesburg	Derrit Loper Poplarville	Cathy Lord Carriere	Jennifer Lossett Picayune
Elaine Lowe Sumrall	Melissa Lowery Columbia	Alicia Lumpkin Poplarville	Felicia Magee Hattiesburg	Paula Magee Poplarville	Terri Magee Bogalusa	Brad Malone Hattiesburg
Marrell Marsh Lumberton	Deborah Martin Perkinston	Tammy Martin Poplarville	Jay Masoner Poplarville	Brady Matthews Poplarville	Sharon Maxwell Brooklyn	Michele McBride Sumrall
Regina McCall Picayune	Prezel McCloud Carson	Sonya McRaney Collins	Shannon McDaniel Columbia	Atlanta McDougle Hattiesburg	Erika McGowan Foxworth	Angela McIntyre Carriere
Katrina McKean Carriere	Pam McKean Nicholson	Kristi McKenzie Purvis	Marie Merritt Lumberton	Patricia Miele Bassfield	Alicia Miles McNeill	Christine Miller Poplarville

Freshmen

Michelle Miller
Picayune

David Mills
Carriere

Darlene Minton
Bay St. Louis

Amanda Mitchell
Picayune

Gewcie Mitchell
Poplarville

Toni Mitchell
Picayune

William Mitchell
Brooklyn

Anita Moffett
Wiggins

Devan Mohr
Hattiesburg

Sharon Monday
Poplarville

Calvin Morales
Picayune

Dana Moran
Picayune

Allen Moree
Columbia

Jean Kliebert and Sharon Koenenn enjoy the day.

Joel Morris
Poplarville

Janne Morrison
Lumberton

Mattie Morris
Hattiesburg

Anita Mosley
Hattiesburg

Jerri Mullins
Columbia

Jamie Murray
Carriere

Teresa Nanney
Petal

Daphne Necaise
Pass Christian

Don Necaise
Pass Christian

Leanne Necaise
Perkinston

Melissa Necaise
Picayune

William Nelson
Poplarville

John Newell
Picayune

Dorothy Nussbaum
Lakeshore

Abrilla Oatis
Bassfield

Dick Ockman
Lumberton

Charlotte Odom
Poplarville

John Odom
Poplarville

Kaye Odom
Lumberton

Synthia Odom
Columbia

Kirk Oge
Bay St. Louis

Berwick Ostheimer
Oak Vale

Michael Owen
Lumberton

Freshmen

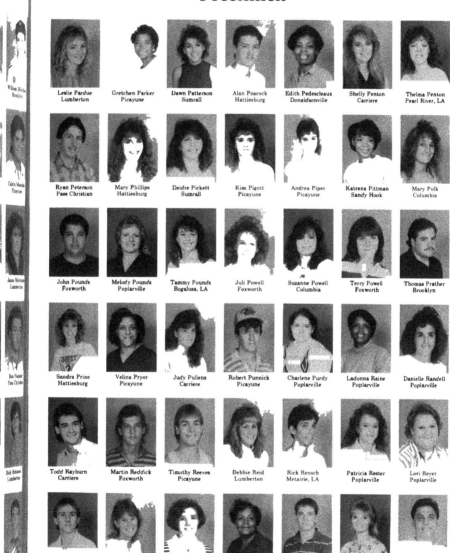

Leslie Pardue Lumberton	Gretchen Parker Picayune	Dawn Patterson Sumrall	Alan Peacock Hattiesburg	Edith Pedescleaux Donaldsonville	Shelly Penton Carriere	Thelma Penton Pearl River, LA
Ryan Peterson Pass Christian	Mary Phillips Hattiesburg	Deidre Pickett Sumrall	Kim Pigott Picayune	Andrea Piper Picayune	Katrena Pittman Sandy Hook	Mary Polk Columbia
John Pounds Foxworth	Melody Pounds Poplarville	Tammy Pounds Bogalusa, LA	Juli Powell Foxworth	Suzanne Powell Columbia	Terry Powell Foxworth	Thomas Prather Brooklyn
Sandra Prine Hattiesburg	Velina Pryor Picayune	Judy Pullens Carriere	Robert Punnick Picayune	Charlene Purdy Poplarville	Ladonna Raine Poplarville	Danielle Randell Poplarville
Todd Rayburn Carriere	Martin Reddick Foxworth	Timothy Reeves Picayune	Debbie Reid Lumberton	Rick Rensch Metairie, LA	Patricia Rester Poplarville	Lori Reyer Poplarville
Paul Reynolds Lumberton	Michelle Rice Purvis	Donna Richardson Pochatoula, LA	Kathleen Richardson Poplarville	Mark Rigney Poplarville	Tabitha Riley Columbia	Daniel Ris Poplarville

171

Freshmen

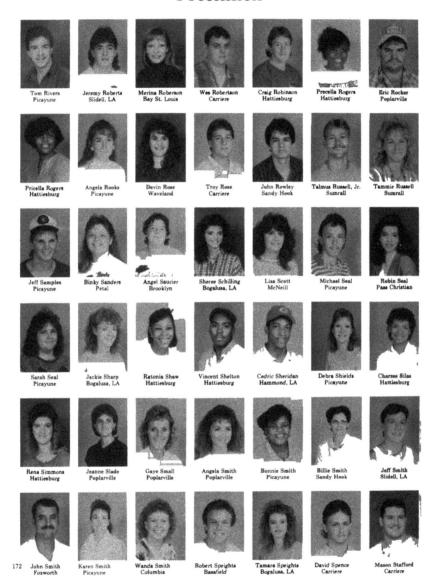

Tom Rivers
Picayune

Jeremy Roberts
Slidell, LA

Merina Roberson
Bay St. Louis

Wes Robertson
Carriere

Craig Robinson
Hattiesburg

Precella Rogers
Hattiesburg

Eric Rocker
Poplarville

Pricella Rogers
Hattiesburg

Angela Rooks
Picayune

Devin Rose
Waveland

Troy Rose
Carriere

John Rowley
Sandy Hook

Talmus Russell, Jr.
Sumrall

Tammie Russell
Sumrall

Jeff Samples
Picayune

Binky Sanders
Petal

Angel Saucier
Brooklyn

Sheree Schilling
Bogalusa, LA

Lisa Scott
McNeill

Michael Seal
Picayune

Robin Seal
Pass Christian

Sarah Seal
Picayune

Jackie Sharp
Bogalusa, LA

Ratonia Shaw
Hattiesburg

Vincent Shelton
Hattiesburg

Cedric Sheridan
Hammond, LA

Debra Shields
Picayune

Charzee Silas
Hattiesburg

Rena Simmons
Hattiesburg

Jeanne Slade
Poplarville

Gaye Small
Poplarville

Angela Smith
Poplarville

Bonnie Smith
Picayune

Billie Smith
Sandy Hook

Jeff Smith
Slidell, LA

172 John Smith
Foxworth

Karen Smith
Picayune

Wanda Smith
Columbia

Robert Speights
Bassfield

Tamara Speights
Bogalusa, LA

David Spence
Carriere

Mason Stafford
Carriere

Freshmen

Eric Stocker
Poplarville

Crisper Stanford
Poplarville

Rusty Stanley
Hattiesburg

Susan Staples
Nicholson

Melody Starr
Picayune

Melissa Steed
Petal

Chad Stewart
Poplarville

Betty Stockstill
Picayune

Tunnie Russell
Sumrall

Bridget Stockstill
Picayune

Rickey Stockstill
Picayune

Tim Stockstill
Carriere

Gwen Stringer
Prentiss

Ques Stringer
Poplarville

Terry Stuart
Bogalusa

Robert Swearingen
Petal

Robin Saul
Pass Christian

Shawna Swilley
Lumberton

Christy Sylvest
Picayune

Jason Tarver
Winnfield, LA

Zelda Tarvin
Hattiesburg

Charnee Silaw
Hattiesburg

Laurie Terrell
Picayune

Lou Thomas
Picayune

Todd Thompson
Bassfield

Alicia Tolar
Columbia

Jeff Smith
Slidell, LA

Roger Tolar
Oak Vale

Craig Toney
Poplarville

Tracy Townsend
Lumberton

Paige Tracey
Pearl River, LA

Mason Stafford
Carriere

Sherie Travis
Poplarville

Mary Trotter
Poplarville

Brad Trussell
Hattiesburg

Ladonna Turner
Poplarville

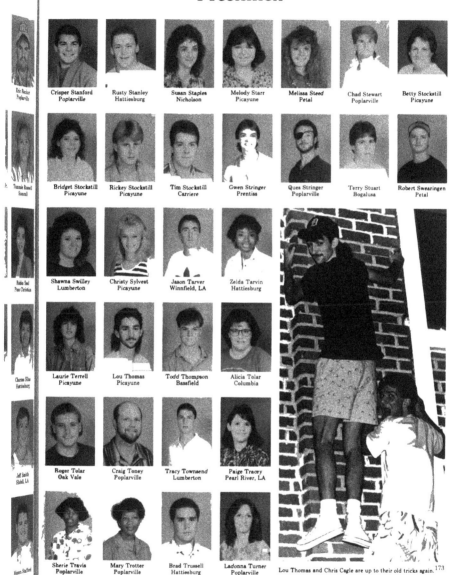

Lou Thomas and Chris Cagle are up to their old tricks again. 173

Freshmen

Richard Ulrich
Picayune

Tina Vanderziel
Columbia

Cortez Vaughn
Picayune

Sarah Walker
Hattiesburg

Alonza Ward
Hattiesburg

Steve Ward
Hattiesburg

Morace Washington
Covington, LA

Janella Watkins
Nicholson

Mark Watts
Columbia

Adrian Weathersby
Newhebron

Huff Hailers, Chris Rankin, David Stromeyer, Lou Thomas, and James Poe, show their stuff.

Reginald Weathersby
Newhebron

Tamala Wells
Hattiesburg

Judy Westfaul
Brooklyn

John Whatley
Brooklyn

Aaron White
Columbia

Laurie White
Columbia

Michael Williamson
Sumrall

Tracy Williford
Lumberton

Mack Womack
Newhebron

Pan Wood
Picayune

Rebecca Wood
Poplarville

Fredrick Worthy
Prentiss

Patsy Wright
Bay St. Louis

Gary Wyman
Pearlington

Ellen Wynne
New Orleans, LA

174

Forrest County Center

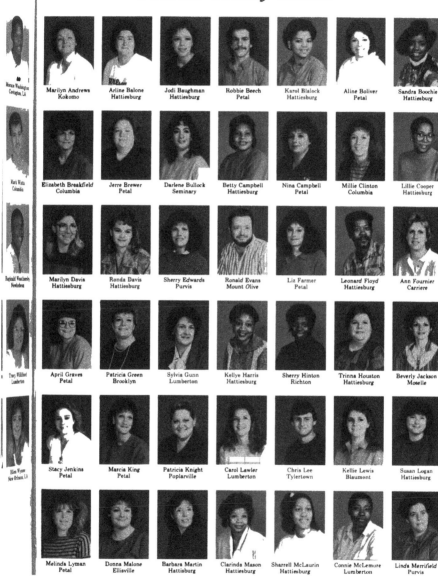

Monroe Washington
Covington, LA

Marilyn Andrews
Kokomo

Arline Balone
Hattiesburg

Jodi Baughman
Hattiesburg

Robbie Beech
Petal

Karol Blalock
Hattiesburg

Aline Boliver
Petal

Sandra Boochie
Hattiesburg

Mark Watts
Columbia

Elizabeth Breakfield
Columbia

Jerre Brewer
Petal

Darlene Bullock
Seminary

Betty Campbell
Hattiesburg

Nina Campbell
Petal

Millie Clinton
Columbia

Lillie Cooper
Hattiesburg

Reginald Weatherby
Newhebron

Marilyn Davis
Hattiesburg

Ronda Davis
Hattiesburg

Sherry Edwards
Purvis

Ronald Evans
Mount Olive

Liz Farmer
Petal

Leonard Floyd
Hattiesburg

Ann Fournier
Carriere

Tracy Williford
Lumberton

April Graves
Petal

Patricia Green
Brooklyn

Sylvia Gunn
Lumberton

Kellye Harris
Hattiesburg

Sherry Hinton
Richton

Trinna Houston
Hattiesburg

Beverly Jackson
Moselle

Ellen Wynne
New Orleans, LA

Stacy Jenkins
Petal

Marcia King
Petal

Patricia Knight
Poplarville

Carol Lawler
Lumberton

Chris Lee
Tylertown

Kellie Lewis
Blaumont

Susan Logan
Hattiesburg

Melinda Lyman
Petal

Donna Malone
Ellisville

Barbara Martin
Hattisburg

Clarinda Mason
Hattiesburg

Sharrell McLaurin
Hattiesburg

Connie McLemure
Lumberton

Linda Merrifield
Purvis

Forrest County Center

Catherine Montoya
Hattiesburg

Jacqueline Moore
Hattiesburg

Stacey Morris
Sumrall

Ella Morris
Hattiesburg

Connie Morrow
Hattiesburg

James Mosely, Jr.
Hattiesburg

Debra Myers
New Augusta

Guwanda Naylor
Hattiesburg

Wilma Oliver
Brooklyn

Lyn Palmer
Petal

Margot Pease
Hattiesburg

Felicia Powell
Hattiesburg

Rosemarie Powell
Hattiesburg

Sylvia Prine
Richton

Lisa Pylan
Petal

Glenda Rankin
Hattiesburg

Pamela Rash
Hattiesburg

Janice Rawls
Hattiesburg

Jo Lynn Rester
Poplarville

Cheri Reus
Hattiesburg

Rondal Rollins
Hattiesburg

Cathy Russell
Bassfield

Mimi Sanders
Hattiesburg

Sachery Sanders
Hattiesburg

Susan Shepherd
Hattiesburg

Rhonda Shoemake
Hattiesburg

Cecelia Simpson
Ovett

Derrick Smith
Hattiesburg

Jacqueline Smith
Hattiesburg

Katherine Smith
Purvis

Patricia Smith
Petal

Debra Stancel
Sumrall

Lori Stamps
Carson

Rhonda Stephens
Sumrall

Jane Stewart
Hattiesburg

176 Willie Stogner
Foxworth

Trish Stogner
Columbia

Selene Stringfellow
Ovett

Marie Sykes
Purvis

William Thompson
Sumrall

Alesia Twillie
Hattiesburg

Sheila Umbdenstock
Hattiesburg

Debra Myers
New Augusta

Lainie Vaughn
Picayune, MS

Alice Vincent
Petal, MS

Pamela Walters
Hattiesburg, MS

Paul Walters
Hattiesburg, MS

Maria Walters
Hattiesburg, MS

Katie Wheat
Poplarville, MS

Karen White
Hattiesburg, MS

Sylvia Prine
Richton

Valorie White
Hattiesburg, MS

Eddie Williams
Lumberton, MS

Deborah Wilson
Columbia, MS

Sherri Wilson
Petal, MS

Roscoe Woullard
Hattiesburg, MS

Hancock County Center

Randal Rollins
Hattiesburg

Darrick Smith
Hattiesburg

Doris Allen
Pass Christian, MS

Florence Asher
Bay St. Louis, MS

Etta Bennett
Carriere, MS

Cathy Burton
Waveland, MS

Cathy Caudill
Bay St. Louis, MS

Darnell Cuevas
Perkinston, MS

Marie Favre
Perkinston, MS

Jane Stewart
Hattiesburg

Wendy Frederick
Bay St. Louis, MS

Tammy Garber
Waveland, MS

Christine Garcis
Bay St. Louis, MS

Diane Grover
Bay St. Louis, MS

Sarah Halford
Bay St. Louis, MS

Georgie Hundle
Bay St. Louis, MS

Jolene Ladner
Pass Christian, MS

Penny Ladner
Pass Christian, MS

Louise Legge
Bay St. Louis, MS

Deborah Mariano
Picayune, MS

Terri Mayne
Waveland, MS

Sandra McGuire
Pearlington, MS

Katherine Miley
Pass Christian, MS

Julie Murphy
Carriere, MS

177

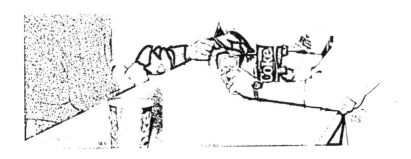

Alana Noonan waits for her next class.

A PRC student poses for a photo from up high.

Johnny Felder works on Mike Clark's truck.

PRC students enjoy lunch in the "Grill."

Chris Cagle and *Lou Thomas phone a friend.*

Wendell Carter *waits for his order from the "Grill."*

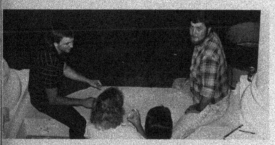

David Knight and *Donnie Brothers enjoy a card game.*

Mitch Biochano *chows down.*

FOOD AND FUN
At Student Center

Scott Cuevas tries his luck at a video game.

Students hang out in P.R.C.'s gameroom on their time off.

A group of P.R.C. students stop off at the student center

Grace Boone awaits her next customer as she chats on the phone.

Rhonda Byrd looks on as Ken Havard receives his order from the grill.

P.R.C. workers wait for the next lunch crowd.

183

Treasures

of the

River

Organizations

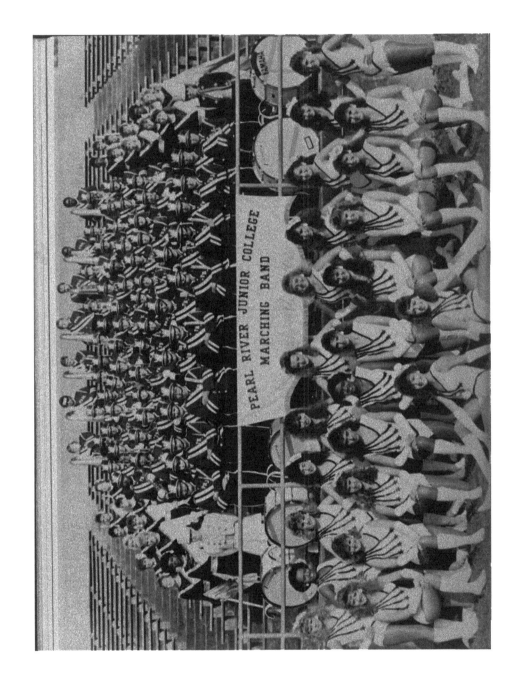

PEARL RIVER JUNIOR COLLEGE MARCHING BAND

Spirit of the River

Archie Rawls has complete control during home basketball games.

Virginia Breland is the 1988-89 Drum Major.

The Spirit of The River performed at all of the home football games.

Riverroad

Riverroad closes their show for the night.

Ruth Pulsifier, Rhonda Bell and Russ Andrus prepare for their next show.

Dawn Patterson and Chuck Harris perform with Riverroad.

(Photos by Tommy Bilbo)

188

Cheerleaders

Front row: Rina Roberson, Sherri Carver, Jennifer Hyatt, and Stacey Johnson. Back row: Sonya McRaney, Angela Haddox, Darla Daniels, Sherri Campbell, Leigh Morris and Shonda Davis.

Norma Hammill
Sponsor

River Navigators

Front row: Jason Dugas, Mark Rigney, Kevin Ladner and Mark Jeanfreau. Back row: Rebecca Wood, Sonya McRaney, Sherri Carver, Marie Merritt, Chysti Doby, Angie Bell, Jeanie Smith and Advisor - Dr. Betty Acken.

NAVIGATOR OFFICERS: Mark Jeanfreau - President, Rebecca Wood - Secretary, Advisor - Dr. Betty Acken, and Chris Schaffer - Vice President.

MASN

Below are members of PRC's chapter of the Mississippi Association of Student Nurses.

Officers

MASN officers are (seated from left) Marilyn Brant, secretary; Sandra Stringer, reporter; and Brenda Entrekin, reporter. Standing are President David Bogle and Treasurer Melanie Watts.

OAADN

At right are members of the Mississippi Organization for Advancement of Associate Degree Nursing.

PBL

Members of Phi Beta Lambda, a business organization, are from left on the first row Laurie Jo Terrell, Gina Lee, Advisor Catherine Merrikin, Tammy Howard, Charmaine Espencheid, Cindy Harvey, Sharon Odom and Debbie Sechrengost. On the second row are Ginger Morris, Sherron Bailey, Angela Pittman, President Rhonda Reid, Vice President Linda Jenkins, Alma Harrington and Tanis Breland. On the third row are 2nd Vice President Jay Able, Advisor Regina Davenport, Anna Gaule, June Noble, Tina Mitchell, Ometrica Ellzey, Lindsey Evans, Leslie Ladner and Janice Pucheu. On the back row are Shirley Smith and Hattie Morris.

Pearls

Seated from left are "String of Pearls" dance team captains Carol Thigpen and Melanie McNabb. On the second row are Bea Bennett, Allison Blades, Jenny Gibson, Tiffany Renfro, Lakeisha Bolton, Michelle Harbeson, Kim McClinton and Teresa Craft. On the third row are Ceci Douglass, Tammy Jenny, Tammy Speights, Tara Whitfield, Christina Hatten and Roxanne Wise. On the back row are Tara Bailey, Rhonda Bilbo, Vicki Seligman, Paula Magee, Dana Dearmann, Kim Koenig, Jennifer Bailey and Yvette Catoire.

Connie Holmes
Advisor

191

Phi Theta Kappa

PTK Executive director Rod Risley was the guest speaker at a club luncheon on campus.

PTK members pictured above are from left on the front row Pam Hollensbe, Angela Haddox, Stephen Trotter, Darla Daniels and Jackie Lawrence. On the second row are advisors Norma Hammill and Ann Morris. On the third row are Rhonda Reid, Sharon Gandy, Margaret LaCavera and Debbie Sechrengost. On the fourth row are Randall Kipker, Tanna McCarty and Sharon Odom. On the fifth row are Scott Suhor, Maja Greulich, Carol Williams and Diana Whisnant. On the back row are Barry McCormick, Russell Hendrix, Chris Schaefer, Anthony King and Wanda Reddick.

New Members

Above are members of the Iota Mu Chapter who were inducted in a fall ceremony. On the first row from left are Maja Greulich, Victoria Piper, Sharon Gandy, Karen Prewett, Lisa Henley, Margaret LaCavera, Rhonda Reid, Debbie Sechrengost, Sharon Odom, Tanna McCarty, Tina Mitchell and Pamela Ladner. On the second row are Jerry Reed, Scott Suhor, Randall Kipker, Berry McCormick, Diana Whisnant, Wanda Reddick, Lucretia Woodson and Cliff Lowe Jr. On the third row are Russell Hendrix, Steve Bounds, Chris Schaefer, Shawn Walker, Jeff Allen and Anthony King.

Yearbook Staff

Newspaper Staff

Front to back: Robin Seal - Wildcat Editor, Donovon Miller, Tiffany Early, Teresa Jones, and Jeff Lockhart, Michael Atkins, not pictured.

Front row: Sharon Koenenn, Tommy Bilbo - Dixie Drawl Editor-in-Chief, Tanya Chapman, Back row: Lou Thomas, Antrice McGill, and Ken Havard.

Advisor - James Stewart

Photographers

First Semester
Susie Seal -
Photo Editor
Matthew Cameron
Stuart Fore
Theresa Jones

Second Semester
Matthew Cameron -
Photo Editor
Theresa Jones

Robin Seal
Spring
Wildcat Editor

Tommy Bilbo
Dixie Drawl Spring
Editor-in-Chief

First Semester Wildcat Staff

Tiffany Early, Kim Koenig - Editor, Chuck Harrison, Tiffany Renfro, Robin Seal and Rebecca Wood.

First Semester Dixie Drawl Staff

Tommy Bilbo - Sports Editor, Jennifer Bochichio, Sheila Johnson, Sharon Koenenn, Johnny Newell, Charles "Earnie" Penton, Moby Smith, Jeff Thompson and Andrea Webb - Editor-in-Chief.

A special thanks goes out to Mrs. Margaret Boone and Amy Bridgers.

Student Council

Student Council Officers for 1988-89 were from left Freshman Representative Jeff Thompson, Sophomore Representative Lynn Seal, Secretary-Treasurer Renee Russell, President Terry Ezell, Freshman President Christina Hatten and Freshman Representative Sherri Carver. Not pictured is Freshman Representative Rebecca Wood.

Freshman Officers

Sophomore Officers

Freshman officers were from left Christina Hatten, president, Sherri Carver, representative, Shonda Davis, secretary, and Stacey Johnson, vice president. Not pictured in Representative Rebecca Wood.

From bottom are sophomore officers Secretary Angela Haddox, Representative Jeff Thompson, President Berry McCormick, Representative Lynn Seal and Vice President Chris Schaefer.

194

VICA

At left are members of, and advisors for PRC's chapter of VICA.

Club Officers

VICA officers pictured from bottom left are Parliamentarian Velina Pryor, Reporter Robert McGee, Treasurer Candace Emerick, Secretary Kimberly Lee, President Elaine Lowe and Historian Shari Mendoza.

195

BSU

Justin Smith, Rich Smith, Chad Stewart, and Dave Lee attend a BSU meeting.

Bill Kirkpatrick talks to a BSU member.

Mark Rigney talks to JoAnn Gerald, Thelma Penton, and Paige Tracey at a BSU meeting.

BSU members pose outside the BSU house for a picture.

COSMO . . . Front row: Samantha Lansdale, Monice Johnson, Tracie Reed, Shwanda Russell, Sena Robertson and Debra Shields. Back row: Jodiy Watkins, Mrs. Pat Amacker, Elaine Lowe, Rhonda Ladner, Sheree Schilling, Melody Pounds, Connie O'Quinn, Kathleen Richardson, Kim Lindsey, Tonia McClendon, Velina Pryor, Dana Lee and Brenda Johnson.

Creative Writing

CREATIVE WRITING . . . Front row: Mrs. Ferguson, Mrs. Patten, Julie Ferril, Willie Altazan, and Eva Mae Henry. Back row: Belinda Pellegrin, Stephen Klark, Stephen Trotter, Dr. Peddicord and Mr. Hoem.

Drama

Christmas at The River

Gretchen Parker and Robert Longino light candles during one of the closing numbers of The Fourth Annual Christmas Vespers, a choral performance.

Russ Andrus, left, and Ernie Penton exit the church at the end of the production. The group held several performances of the Christmas Vespers in the local area.

Dr. Patricia Malone (at left) waits for her cue to began playing her oboe, while Reuben McDowell accompanies the choir on the piano.

The Pearl River Singers, PRC's choral group, performs under the direction of Dr. Mark Malone at the First Baptist Church of Poplarville.

(Photos by James Stewart)

Afro-American Club

The Afro-American Club of Pearl River Community College rehearses for their performance of the black history program. To the right are Darlene Acker and Gretchen Parker, singers with the club's choir.

Derrit Loper, the club's president, discusses the arrangement of music, for the program, with club musician Scotty Tyrone (far right). Katrina Pittman (below), practices for the program by singing her song for the club members.

Ray Hampton (below right), the choirs director, directs the groups rehearsal session.

Breaking ground: Work begins on technology center

Helping with the ground breaking for the technology center were (from left) Don Welsh, vocational/technical director; Herman Lee, county administrator; Bill Blasingame, division director, Resource Management Coordination, State Department; Dr. James Sones, dean of vocational/technical affairs; D.R. Davis, chancery clerk; Tommy Pearson, supervisor; Buster Moody, supervisor; Charles Stewart, supervisor; Jimmy Ladner, supervisor; Dr. Thomas Blakeney, PRC board chairman; Kathryn Moody, board member; Jerry Burge, board member; Fred Wagner, architect; Pat W. Sellers, Jay-Van Company; and Ron Holmes, PRC business manager.

The Jay-Van Co. was in charge of construction of the building, and worker began pouring the foundation in January. The building was expected to b completed within 10 months.

(Photos by James Stewart)

Workers smooth the concrete forming the foundation of the $2 million building.

Although it may appear so, this man was not left to be stuck in the slab. The brace in his hands is used to patch rough spots in the wet concrete.

Concrete pouring activities (pictured at left) were delayed for a while in January when winter rains moved in.

203

Chris Price, Scott Daniels and John Alexander take a break.

Rodney Sampson hard at work.

Vo-tech students wait for their next class.

Vo-Tech Classes

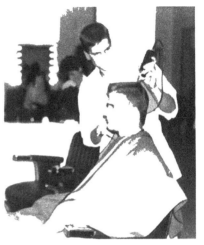

Otis Mitchell gives Jason Roland a haircut.

Robbie Johnson and Mike Barnes do exercise with vo-tech equipment.

David Johnson and Joe Higginbotham check test circuits.

Roese Neves and Eldon Buel check out equipment.

Academic Classes

Kathleen Bogle talks to her class about graphs.

Academic students listen to a class lecture.

Mrs. Roane assists a P.R.C. student.

y Vega and *Darron Stamant get started at the computers.*

iee Hoem discusses journals with his English Comp. II class.

Mardi Gras At The River

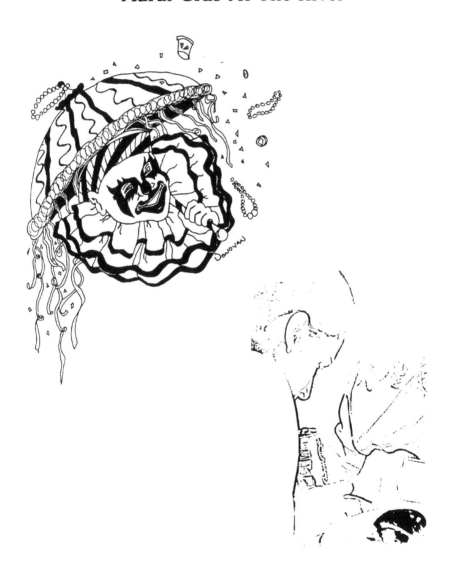

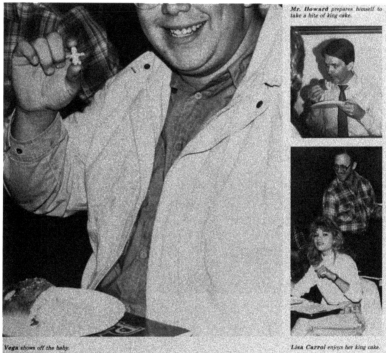

Mr. Howard prepares himself to take a bite of king cake.

Vega shows off the baby.

Lisa Carrol enjoys her king cake.

PRC's Band participates in the Bay St. Louis parade.

Hitch a ride on the PRC Bandwagon.

The Queen waves to the crowd along highway 90 in Bay St. Louis.

Catch those beads!

PRC's Band plays in the Bay parade.

211

P.R.C. Blood Drive

Russ Andrus smiles as he donates blood at the February 1st blood drive.

Eddie Ladner looks around while donating blood.

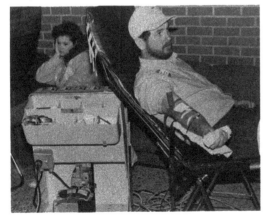

212

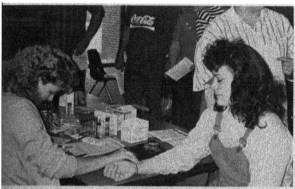

Debra Dailey has her pulse taken before donating blood.

Chuck "Jersey" Bablowski gives blood.

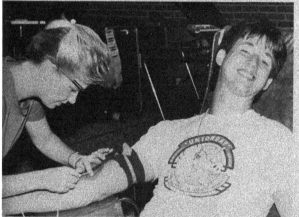

Donate Blood

United Blood Services
A DIVISION OF BLOOD SYSTEMS, INC.
A NONPROFIT CORPORATION

Somebody needs it every day

NURSES COLLECT
124 PINTS OF BLOOD

The Mississippi Association of Student Nurses' blood drive, held in Marion Hall lobby, February 1, collected 124 pints of blood for use in Mississippi hospitals.

"The blood drive was a great success," said Sandra Stringer, reporter for MASN.

Out of 145 donors, 124 pints of blood were collected. The collection exceeded the clubs goal of 120 pints.

20 MASN students and faculty members assisted the Mississippi Blood Services Inc. with the blood drive.

"Although I observed some apprehensive faces, all in all it was fun, thanks to all the brave students who donated and to those who helped," said Stringer.

A raffle was also held for a two pound box of Russell Stover valentine candy donated by the Pearl River Drug Company in Poplarville. Diane Whisnant, of Poplarville, was the winner of the raffle.

A Blood Services technician takes Margret La Cavera's blood pressure at the February 1 blood drive.

A nursing student prepares Russell Andrus to give blood.

One of the technicians with the Blood Services Inc. prepares blood bags for use.

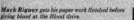

Student nurses get students prepared for giving blood.

Mark Rigney gets his paper work finished before giving blood at the Blood drive.

The best part of the day . . . going home. There are approximately 300 stu-dents at the "River" who use the buses as their transportation to and from col-lege.

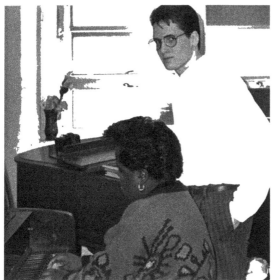

P.R.C.'s
Music
Room

John Wilkinson looks on as Christine plays a few notes.

Kim Bonds practices playing the piano.

217

Robert Purvis works quietly at his computer.

Michael Lucas types away at his computer.

otos by Matthew Cameron)

J. Trotter gets some assistance with her computer.

Debra Bass checks her typing for errors.

Angela Barret uses the new computers in the business technology class.

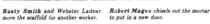

(Photos by James Stewart)

A section is cut in the bricks for workers to install a new door.

Eric Nixon works from a scaffold.

The Styles Of
The River

This PRC student shows off his new haircut, which was done in the River's barbershop.

Below is Johnny Felder's four wheel drive Toyota, "Splash." It is easily recognizable with its plum crazy (purple) background and vivid tangerine orange splashes.

*hese cool guys - T.C. Carter and his friend, Keith, are ready to be photographed. Keith is sporting the lat-
t fad, ripped jeans. This is a very popular item around campus.*

*sother thing that's hot is personalized license plates. These "tags" spell out many
fferent things. Some have phrases, others have names, initials, or mottos. Whatever
e case may be, each tag makes the owner's car an original.*

This is an example of one of the front tags on campus.

Below is Jamie Favre's Toyota 4x4, "Sho Off." It has a hydraulic tilt lift as demonstrated.

This is an example of a low rider. Low riders are the very latest thing in trucks. This one belongs to Mike Clark. It has a tan background with pastel trim.

Weight Training

No Pain - No Gain

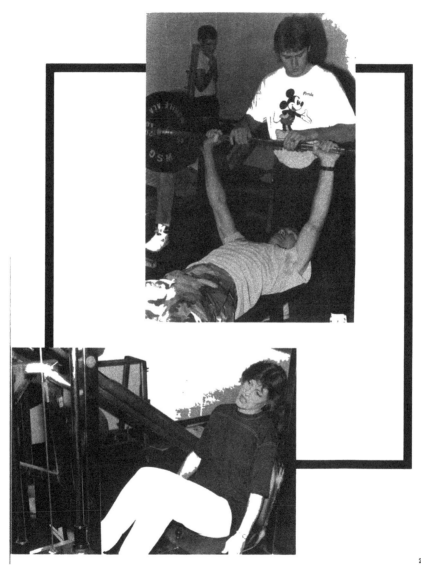

At right J.W. Sones, assistant intra-
murals director keeps an eye on the
game room.

Joe Woods and Richard Santiago
(above) watch ping pong players.

Above competitors in a pool tournament size up their competition.

Wayne Marisco and Greg Ladner prepare for the rain.

Terri Magee and JoEll Perry dissect a frog in Biology.

Hope Seal, Craig Ladner, Dennis Lizana, Patricia Rester, Mike Grisham and Rebecca Rester wait for the Pass Christian parade to begin.

Marsha Pullens and *Lynn Hagenson rest after a halftime performance.*

Nancy Byers takes a piano break.

Rhonda McCardle, April Austin, Scott Suhor, Randy Kipker and Melinda Walley cruise around campus in Randy's convertible.

Chris Cagle reads over his notes for a test.

A garbage truck waits below while repairs were being done on Huff Hall.

Christine Miller talks to a friend while Mike Simms looks on.

Wanda Butler and friend walk across the parking lot to class.

231

Special Events

Robert Noland and Robin Lyle, members of the Christian music group Gabriel, talk with members of the audience after their performance, which was sponsored by the BSU.

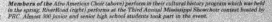

Members of the Afro American Choir (above) perform in their cultural history program which was held in the spring. RiverRoad (right) performs at the Third Annual Mississippi Showchoir contest hosted by PRC. Almost 300 junior and senior high school students took part in the event.

The band Odyssey took first place in the spring talent show. Kneeling is Travis Kennedy, and standing from left are Chad Stewart, Thomas Strebeck, Michael Byrd and Terry Ezell.

Clay Jenkinson, a 17th century scholar, portrayed Thomas Jefferson in a series of lectures coordinated by PRC.

SPARC Valentine's Day Dance

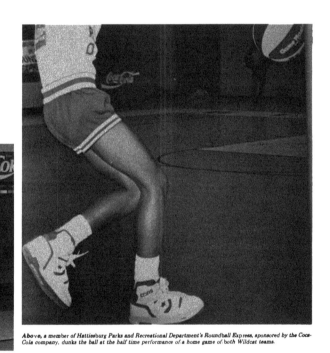

Above, a member of Hattiesburg Parks and Recreational Department's Roundball Express, sponsored by the Coca-Cola company, dunks the ball at the half time performance of a home game of both Wildcat teams.

Express members wait for their que to perform.

To the left, Express members dazzle the on-looking fans with their talents. The Roundball Express is comprised of Hattiesburg area kids.

Below, Tim Lee, an intern in the Public Relations Department of Pearl River Community College, waits to announce the second half of the game.

Below left, W.C. Rivers, portrayed by Rich Smith, gets to know a little fan better.

Single Parent/Displaced Homemaker Offic|

Cathy Mitchell (top left) does some homework between classes.   *Gail DeJarnette (top right) signs in.*   *Gerry Bostic and Mary Mallery (above) work class assignments.*

Above Beverly Tynes, director of the Single Parent/Displaced Homemakers program, which helps adult students make the transition to college life, takes care of some paper work. At left Martha Brooks Brown, a counselor with the program, helps Lynn Schaller with some homework.

Spring '88

Above are Stacy Walker (left) and Robert Lott. Walker won the 19 Mathematics/Physics Department Academic Achievement Awa which was presented by Lott.

Above is Lamont Pearson (right) and Dena O'Bannon. Pearson was the recipient of the 1988 PRC Journalism Award, which was presented by O'Bannon.

Below are Joey Tatum of Picayune and Dr. Mil Hammill, dean of student affairs. Tatum was th recipient of the Pearl River Community Colle Award.

To the right are Debbie Kinard (right) and Steve Howard. Kinard was the recipient of the 1988 Computer Science Award, which was presented by Howard.

At left are Millie Wilks of Columbia, and Lee Mock of York, Ala., recipients of the J.J. Holcomb Award as the female and male athletes of the 1987-88 school year.

238

Awards '88

To the right are Angie King (right) of Lumberton and Dr. James Barnes, PRC science instructor. King received the Science Department Academic Achievement Award.

Above are Francis Huch (left) of Picayune and Suzanne Hodnett of Carriere (right), recipients of the Communications Department Academic Achievement Awards. The awards were presented by Mike Knippers, PRC speech instructor (center).

To the right are Donna Gilbert (left) of Prentiss and Delora Smith (right) of Poplarville, recipients of the Nursing Department Academic Achievement Awards, which were presented by Charlotte Odom (center), director of the ADN program.

Pictured below are the recipients of several Delta Psi Omega Awards. They are, front row from left, Ethel Parker Johnson of Bay St. Louis, Best Actress - children's play and Best Crew Member - dinner theater; Lisa Batson of Poplarville, Best Actress - dinner theater; Connie Holmes, advisor; Kim Turnage of Columbia, Outstanding Crew Member (2 years); Shannon Cagle of Hattiesburg, Best Crew Member - children's play; Tracey Smith of Poplarville, Outstanding Delta Psi Omega Award. Back row from left are John Turner of Lumberton, Outstanding Drama Award; Darrin Daniels of Poplarville, Outstanding Delta Psi Omega Award; Daniel Dorion of Bay St. Louis, Best Actor - dinner theater; and Chris King of Carriere, Best Actor - children's play.

To the left is John Padgett of Picayune. Padgett was recognized for placing first in the drama division at the Mississippi Junior College Creative Writing Association's Annual Convention. Padgett is the first writer at PRC to receive such an honor.

239

Awards

Above are Rhonda Breeland (left) and Dottie Bisland. Rhonda Breeland, a major in Business Computer Applications, placed third in the machine transcription competition at the Future Business Leaders of America State Leadership Conference.

Above are the members of the Dixie Drawl staff, the free student newspaper at PRC. The Dixie Drawl won the Mississippi Junior/Community College Press Association's General Excellence Award in their division for the eleventh consecutive year.

Below are the winners of the PRC Vocational Awards. Pictured front row from left are Wilmon Henderson of Nicholson, Machine Shop Award; Jackie Lee of Poplarville, Cosmetology Award; Bryan Dixon of Sandy Hook, Electricity Award; John Daley of Bassfield, Heating, Air Conditioning and Refrigeration Award; Lionel Ellison of New Orleans, La., Carpentry Award. Back row from left Steven Barrett of Purvis, Masonry Award; Kevin Herrin of Purvis, Diesel Mechanics Award; Thomas Hill of Poplarville, Citizenship Award; and Keith Cavaliere of Picayune, Automotive Mechanics Award. Not Pictured is Donald Howell of Pearl River, La., Welding Award.

Above are the winners of the Secretarial Science Awards. From left are Rosemary Miller, of Picayune, winner of the (two-year) Business and Office Award; Cheryl Morrow of Purvis, winner of the (two-year) Medical Office Award; and Connie Lee of Prentiss, winner of the (one-year) Business and Office Award. Nancy Reagan, business instructor, presented the awards.

Below are the winners of the PRC Technical Award Winners. From left are Bret Steelman of Carriere, Drafting and Design Technology Award; Byron Matthews of Carriere, Computer Operations Technology Award; Timothy Davis of Poplarville, Computer Programming Technology Award; Ken Cowart of Poplarville, Marketing/Management Technology Award; and Bret Barnes of McNeill, Electronics Technology Award.

Faculty Awards '88

Above: Ann Donnell of Hattiesburg, a nursing instructor at the Poplarville campus, was presented the "Academic Instructor of the Year" award by Dr. Ted J. Alexander.

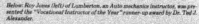
Below: Roy Jones (left) of Lumberton, an Auto mechanics instructor, was presented the "Vocational Instructor of the Year" runner-up award by Dr. Ted J. Alexander.

Above: Doris Allen of Pass Christian, a practical nursing instructor at the Hancock County Vo-Tech Center, was presented the "Vocational Instructor of the Year" award by Dr. Ted J. Alexander.

Below: Special recognition was given to PRC cafeteria employees Mary Graham (left) and Olivia Bender, both of Poplarville. Bender and Graham have been working at the college for the past 38 years.

Faculty Awards '88

Ann Morris of Poplarville, a business technology instructor, was presented the "Technical Instructor of the Year Award" by Dr. Ted J. Alexander.

C.B. McDonald (left) of Poplarville was presented the "Service/Trade Staff Member of the Year" award by Dr. Ted J. Alexander.

Barbara Wise, Poplarville secretary at the main campus, was presented "Support Staff of the Year" runner-up award.

Faculty Awards '88

Dr. James Sones (left) of Poplarville, dean of vocational technical education, was presented the Administrative (non-teaching) "Professional of the Year" award by Dr. Ted J. Alexander.

Janet Edwards, Purvis secretary at Lamar County Center was named "Support Staff Member of the Year."

Dr. Willis Lott (left) of Poplarville, was presented the administrative (non-teaching) "Professional of the Year" runner-up award by Dr. Ted J. Alexander. Dr. Lott is the academic dean.

Hancock County Center

Alvin Bourgeois, director of the center, goes over some paperwork in his office.

Marie Favre, at left, types a memo, while Doris Allen, a practical nursing instructor, checks a student's notebook above.

types a memo, while Ben
using Interactive, check i
done

Forrest County Center

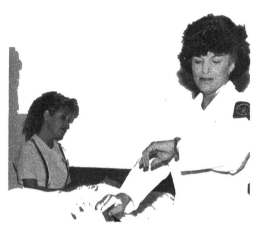

Cynthia
Lloyd
Business
Computers
Application.

Francis Long
Teacher's
Aid

Vicki Polk
Secretary

247

College Publications Staffs Hard At Work

Antrice McGill runs off a copy of her next newspaper article.

Robin Seal, the Wildcat Editor, sorts through pictures for the yearbook.

Tiffany Early checks over a yearbook page for errors.

Sharon Koenenn works on writing up her next article for The Dixie Drawl.

Tonya Chapman looks back over her latest article for the newspaper.

Tommy Bilbo, The Dixie Drawl's Editor-in-Chief, uses the light machine to assist him in his work.

Jeff Lockhart checks over a list of names.

Theresa Jones helps out with the yearbook.

Snapshots

(Photo by Robin Seal)

Call

G.M. Ables
Columbia

Charlotte D. Aborom
Hattiesburg

Ruth B. Abram
Columbia

Donna M. Abshire
Slidell, LA

Crystal Acker
Waveland

Darlene M. Acker
Bay St. Louis

Furnell A. Acker
Pearlington

Larry R. Acker
Pearlington

Kimberly Adams
Angie, LA

Rita M. Adams
Picayune

Donna K. Adcox
Picayune

Terrell W. Adcox
Poplarville

Walter A. Adcox
Bogalusa, LA

James R. Agent
Purvis

Joseph G. Albe, Jr.
Waveland

Mary B. Alritton
Columbia

Vicky L. Alcaien
Bay St. Louis

Alan F. Alderman
Picayune

Bryan W. Alexander
Poplarville

Cynthia J. Alexander
Picayune

Edwin Alexander
Angie, LA

John M. Alexander
Picayune

Marsha S. Alexander
Carriere

Melvin D. Alexander
Carriere

Constance A. Alford
Foxworth

Judy C. Alford
Poplarville

Rosalyn Alford
Foxworth

Frances P. Alison
Picayune

Brenda C. Alleman
Waveland

Annie Allen
Angie, LA

Jeff L. Allen
Carson

Joey Allen
Columbia

Joey M. Allen
Columbia

Dristi R. Allen
Carriere

Pamela F. Allen
Poplarville

Ronald S. Allen
Lumberton

Timothy E. Allen
Columbia

Charles R. Allman
Lumberton

Willie J. Altazan
Poplarville

Chellie R. Amacker
Carriere

Glenn A. Amacker
Carriere

Michelle L. Amacker
Poplarville

Bradley S. Anderson
Purvis

James R. Anderson
Lumberton

John G. Anderson
Prentiss

John M. Anderson
Lumberton

Marlene Anderson
Poplarville

Sherlyl M. Anderson
Hattiesburg

Susan Anderson
Poplarville

Shedric R. Andrews
Brooklyn

Russell N. Andrus
Petal

Kathrine A. Aplin
Hattiesburg

Anthony T. Applewhite
Bassfield

Chastan M. Applewhite
Poplarville

Onita K. Applewhite
Bassfield

Tressie J. Applewhite
Poplarville

Idus O. Arcement
Carriere

Jerry D. Ard
Petal

Debrah S. Arrington
Petal

Christopher J. Artigues
Bay St. Louis

Mary E. Arvel
Donaldsville, LA

Vanessa K. Ash
Hattiesburg

Donna M. Ashe
Carriere

Kim A. Ashe
Poplarville

Michael M. Atkins
Gunnison

William J. Atwood
Lumberton

Janice R. Aultman
Hattiesburg

Dawn D. Austill
Pearlington

April L. Austin
Wiggins

Heidi E. Austin
Wiggins

Shawn Avery
Slidell, LA

Charles A. Babiowski
Turnersville, NJ

Robert P. Backus
Hattiesburg

Fara Bailey
Lumberton

Jennifer L. Bailey
Lumberton

Reginald Bailey
Picayune

Sherron R. Bailey
Foxworth

Boris E. Baker
Poplarville

Donna G. Baker
Petal

Gene A. Baker
Picayune

Nichelle T. Baker
Picayune

Sandra Baker
Oakvale

Richard Baldwin
Poplarville

Angela C. Barker
Columbia

Bobbie W. Barber
Columbia

Tracy M. Bardwell
Lumberton

Johnnye M. Barilleaux
Bay St. Louis

Naomi R. Barilleaux
Bay St. Louis

Angela A. Barker
Picayune

Tonia L. Barker
Covington, LA

Barbara A. Barnes
Prentiss

Calvin D. Barnes
Columbia

Donald R. Barnes
Bassfield

James M. Barnes
Poplarville

Kristen L. Barnes
Carriere

Thomas P. Barnes
Prentiss

Harry M. Barnett, III
Poplarville

Marjorie L. Barnett
Lafayette, LA

Mitchell H. Barnett
Columbia

Anthony Barney
Hattiesburg

Angela M. Barrett
Lumberton

Steven R. Barrett
Purvis

William H. Barrett
Lumberton

Carol M. Baskin
Hattiesburg

Deborah J. Bass
Prentiss

John K. Bass
Hattiesburg

Donald C. Bates
Lumberton

Timothy J. Batzli
Carriere

Shannon Baughman
Poplarville

Terry L. Baughman
Poplarville

Christy L. Baxter
Picayune

Donna M. Baxter
Poplarville

Melinda G. Baylis
Columbia

Cassandra M. Bazor
Perkinston

Brenda S. Beach
Lumberton

Connie R. Beacht
Picayune

Rhonda Beall
Lumberton

Patsy R. Beard
Columbia

Trena Beard
Prentiss

Kelli R. Beasley
Hattiesburg

Myra Beckham
Poplarville

Carolyn D. Beech
Picayune

Donna C. Beech
Picayune

John S. Beith
Carriere

Angela A. Bell
Columbia

Carolyn J. Bell
Picayune

Kelly S. Bell
Bay St. Louis

Kenneth M. Bell
Bay St. Louis

Shannon C. Bell
Picayune

Joseph S. Bello
Pearlington

Charles J. Bennett
Pearlington

Charlotte B. Bennett
Picayune

Holly L. Bennett
Picayune

Michael D. Bennett
Nicholson

Karen D. Berger
Lumberton

Stacy L. Bergeron
Picayune

Todd M. Bergeron
Baton Rouge, LA

Antonio R. Berry
Hattiesburg

Renee P. Berry
Prentiss

Ruby L. Berry
Bassfield

Rhonda M. Best
Picayune

Ron T. Bester
Poplarville

Cheryl F. Bethley
Hattiesburg

Mitch C. Biancato
Metairie, LA

Linda Bickham
Bogalusa, LA

Elizabeth V. Bilbo
Carriere

Gloria J. Bilbo
Lumberton

John L. Bilbo
Picayune

Monica L. Bilbo
Bay St. Louis

Rhonda L. Bilbo
Bay St. Louis

Thomas D. Bilbo, Jr.
Carriere

Ray A. Billeaud, Jr.
Picayune

Betty Bingham
Hattiesburg

Jane M. Bira
Poplarville

Kathy D. Bishop
Lumberton

Kelli S. Blackmon
Picayune

Rosalyne Blackston
Hattiesburg

Marcia D. Blackwell
Hattiesburg

Allison D. Blades
Picayune

Nella Blair
Picayune

Taren A. Breland
Pearlington

Virginia A. Breland
Petal

Wanda F. Breland
Carriere

Michael A. Bremer
Bogalusa, LA

Thomas L. Bremer
Bogalusa, LA

Dianna A. Breshears
Lumberton

Margaret C. Brewer
Picayune

Rhonda M. Brewer
Morgantown

Timothy E. Brewer
Morgantown

Tyra J. Brewer
Picayune

Wade Bridgeman
Slidell, LA

Allen D. Bringedahl
Lumberton

Eric G. Brister
Bogalusa, LA

Henry D. Brister
Kokomo

Cynthia L. Brooks
Poplarville

Amanda L. Broom
Sumrall

Radonna L. Broom
Columbia

Jr. Susan L. Broome
Sumrall

Bryan A. Brothers
Purvis

Donald W. Brothers
Purvis

Charietta C. Brown
Hattiesburg

Corey S. Brown
Columbia

Crystal L. Brown
Wiggins

Juanita H. Brown
Lumberton

Lynda L. Brown
Columbia

Mark A. Brown
Columbia

Robert E. Brown
Hattiesburg

Terri Ann Brown
Lumberton

David J. Brownlow
Poplarville

Margie Brun
Lumberton

Judith M. Bruno
Bay St. Louis

Tommy F. Bryant, Jr.
Columbia

Linda F. Bryant
Bogalusa, LA

Wayne E. Bryd
Purvis

Melissa L. Buckley
Columbia

Joyce A. Bullock
Hattiesburg

Kenneth Bullock
Picayune

Sharon E. Bullock
Lumberton

Victoria L. Bullock
Columbia

Yvette M. Bullock
Petal

Connie S. Burge
Carriere

Debora F. Burge
Carriere

Eleanor Burge
Carriere

June L. Burge
Picayune

Karen R. Burge
Picayune

Kathy S. Burge
Poplarville

Leo R. Burge
Carriere

Randolph W. Burge
Picayune

Ronda M. Burge
Picayune

Shayne S. Burgess
Picayune

Laurie S. Burkett
Bogalusa, LA

Paula J. Burkhalter
Picayune

Wanda L. Burkhalter
Lumberton

Kitty Jo Burnette
Carriere

Marty D. Burns
Covington, LA

Monica L. Burns
Carriere

Patrick S. Burns
Bassfield

Corey Burton
Poplarville

William L. Bush
Columbia

Joseph A. Busha
Hattiesburg

Alison S. Butler
Carriere

Kenny H. Byers
Hattiesburg

Nancy L. Byers
Hattiesburg

Shannon L. Bynum
Purvis

Stephen T. Bynum
Purvis

Cecilia D. Byrd
Picayune

Charles M. Byrd, Jr.
Picayune

Martha L. Byrd
Lumberton

Paula W. Byrd
Carriere

Steven W. Byrd
Picayune

Michael Byro
Gulfport

Beverly L. Cagins
Columbia

Floyd R. Cagins
Columbia

Chris V. Cagle
Columbia

Jeffrey W. Caillouet
Carriere

Patricia A. Callender
Nicholson

Matthew J. Cameron
Bay St. Louis

Theresa T. Cameron
Lumberton

Annette M. Campbell
Poplarville

Eric R. Campbell
Sumrall

Glen T. Campbell
Lumberton

Kelly M. Campbell
Carriere

Kirby R. Campbell
Poplarville

Sherrie L. Campbell
Purvis

Paul D. Cantrell
Poplarville

Sheila A. Carbonette
Nicholson

Donald W. Carlan
Carriere

Stephen Carlson
Carriere

Charles M. Carney
Monticello

Chuck M. Carney
Monticello

Jason A. Carney
Kokomo

Julie Carr
Lumberton

Wanda F. Carr
Poplarville

Cindy J. Carroll
Angie, LA

Lisa D. Carroll
Picayune

Stacey L. Carroll
Angie, LA

Darriell D. Carter
Picayune

Desma S. Carter
Picayune

Erica D. Carter
Hattiesburg

Evelyn L. Carter
Hattiesburg

Gibson J. Carter
Bay St. Louis

Mildred L. Carter
Hattiesburg

Sherrie J. Carter
Lumberton

Terry B. Carter
Slidell, LA

Wendell Carter
Atlanta, GA

Linda A. Carver
Bay St. Louis

Nathan A. Carver
Bay St. Louis

Sherri K. Carver
Waveland

Yvette S. Catoire
Poplarville

Dawn M. Cecil
Picayune

Phyllis A. Cedotal
Bogalusa, LA

Brenda M. Cerniglia
Poplarville

Samuel V. Cerniglia
Bogalusa, LA

Norris P. Chaisson
Pearl River, LA

Monique A. Chaix
Carriere

Duane J. Champagne
Picayune

Kirk J. Champagne
Franklin, LA

Debra K. Chandler
Sumrall

Tonya R. Chapman
Hattiesburg

Maria A. Chatman
Hattiesburg

Jagade W. Chifici
Bay St. Louis

Benny E. Childs
Poplarville

Tommy A. Chisolm
Carriere

Wendy M. Cieutat
Bay St. Louis

Christopher P. Clark
Petal

Deborah Clark
Poplarville

Kristine A. Clark
Waveland

Michael S. Clark
Foxworth

Patrick L. Clark
Hattiesburg

Rodney S. Clark
Hattiesburg

Tommy K. Clark
Angie, LA

Wallace J. Clark
Acadia, LA

Deborah A. Clarke
Bogalusa, LA

Gracie Clay
Nicholson

Chris W. Clinton
Sumrall

Sheri J. Clunan
Poplarville

Andrew J. Coblentz
Carriere

Curtis W. Cochran
Hattiesburg

Kristi Cole
Hattiesburg

Alana J. Collins
Columbia

Dawne E. Collins
Hattiesburg

Richard M. Collum
Brooklyn

Shawn Conerly
Covington, LA

Tonya L. Conerly
Kokomo

Camille A. Conner
Hattiesburg

Jammie G. Cook
Columbia

Johnette Cook
Wiggins

Kimberly D. Cook
Poplarville

Kimberly S. Cook
Picayune

Tracey M. Cook
Hattiesburg

Jason F. Cooksey
Carriere

Thomas R. Cool
Bay St. Louis

Therese R. Cooper
Carriere

Donna J. Corkern
Bogalusa, LA

Cynthia P. Cotton
Carriere

Brian D. Courtney
Bassfield

Jeffrey A. Courville
Picayune

Eleanor Couturier
Poplarville

Michael J. Cowan
Hattiesburg

Donna M. Cowart
Picayune

Cami Cox
Columbia

Christi J. Cox
Picayune

Kimberly S. Cox
Bay St. Louis

Chris D. Craddock
Picayune

Lucille Craft
Hattiesburg

Teresa A. Craft
Picayune

Tiffanie D. Craft
Picayune

Barbara Cranmer
Bay St. Louis

Jimmy E. Crawford
Picayune

Albert K. Creel
McNeill

Shannon C. Creel
Carriere

Rose Crider
Picayune

Stephen D. Crocker
Lumberton

Tammy E. Croney
Picayune

Deborah A. Crouchet
Picayune

Philip S. Crowley
Purvis

Richard A. Cudd, Jr.
Picayune

Anthony S. Cuevas
Poplarville

Colleen F. Cuevas
Pass Christian

Michael D. Cullop
Columbia

Charles E. Culpepper
Poplarville

Amy Cumberland
Poplarville

John J. Cumberland
Poplarville

Andra L. Cutrer
Picayune

Bryan P. Daley
Bassfield

Deborah L. Daley
Carson

Michael D. Daley
Carson

Shelly R. Daley
Bassfield

Agnes P. Daniels
Carriere

Belinda F. Daniels
Nicholson

Darla Y. Daniels
Poplarville

David Daniels
Columbia

Eddie D. Daniels
Hattiesburg

James I. Daniels
carriere

John E. Daniels
Carriere

Renitta Daniels
Poplarville

Sheila C. Daniels
Poplarville

Deborah D. Darby
Hattiesburg

Michael J. Darby
Hattiesburg

Noah C. Daspit
Pearlington

Sean S. Dassau
Carriere

Anna D. Daughdrill
Poplarville

Glenda L. Daughdrill
Hattiesburg

Jason Daughtrey
Petal

Beverly Davis
Poplarville

Brian K. Davis
Poplarville

Cathy D. Davis
Picayune

Daphne M. Davis
Picayune

David S. Davis
Poplarville

Deborah L. Davis
Picayune

Dina K. Davis
Picayune

Donna A. Davis
McNeill

Donna M. Davis
Poplarville

Dorothy L. Davis
Picayune

Douglas W. Davis
Columbia

Gary S. Davis
Sumrall

J. Jeff Davis
Collins

Joseph Davis
Bogue Chitto

Leandrea I. Davis
Lumberton

Michael S. Davis
Picayune

Nazli L. Davis
Bay St. Louis

Nina R. Davis
Poplarville

Peggy N. Davis
Poplarville

Scott C. Davis
Hattiesburg

Shannon M. Davis
Hattiesburg

Sherry A. Davis
Picayune

Shonda K. Davis
Picayune

Theresa A. Davis
Carriere

Thomas J. Davis
Bassfield

Zella S. Davis
Picayune

Anna M. Dawkins
Picayune

Donald E. Dawsey, II
Pearlington

Carl M. Day
Columbia

Veronica L. Dear
Picayune

Dana M. Dearman
Purvis

Ina J. Dearman
Wiggins

Warren D. Dearman
Purvis

Wendy J. Deben
Bay St. Louis

Dennis S. Debrow
Purvis

Patricia A. Dedeaux
Picayune

Sandra A. Deere
Picayune

Carlton T. Defiore
Carriere

Cynthia Delahoussaye
Pearl River, LA

Frank Denard, Jr.
Hattiesburg

Scott Deters
Picayune

Dennis D. Devore
Carriere

Daisy M. Dewease
Purvis

Angie D. Dickerson
Bay St. Louis

Amanda J. Dickinson
Hattiesburg

Jo A. Dickinson
Hattiesburg

Nicholas Difabrizio
Slidell, LA

Larry P. Dillard, Jr.
Carnere

Allice Dillon
Columbia

Irene Dillon
Foxworth

Cindy H. Dixon
Carriere

Earnestine L. Dixon
Prentiss

Rachell Y. Dixon
Hattiesburg

Karen D. Dobson
Purvis

Lawrence K. Dobson
Purvis

Chrysti S. Doby
Pearlington ´ -

Anna C. Dodd
Picayune

Jill A. Dodd
Picayune

Sherman C. Dodd
Picayune

Richard B. Donegan
Hattiesburg

Daniel S. Dorion
Bay St. Louis

Mary H. Dorr
Carriere

Debbie D. Dorsey
Bay St. Louis

Jennifer E. Dossett
Picayune

Tony A. Dossett
Picayune

Richard Dossett
Picayune

Robyn L. Douglass
Bogalusa, LA

Cecilia A. Douglass
Lumberton

Lorie E. Downes
Nicholson

Sybil L. Downes
Picayune

Sybil M. Downes
Picayune

William S. Downes
Nicholson

Melinda A. Downing
Sumrall

Maurice Dozier
Macon, GA

William K. Drennan
Picayune

Marla M. Dreyer
Poplarville

Felicia L. Drummond
Sumrall

Chris J. Dubois
Eunice, LA

Debra C. Dubose
Lumberton

Rhonda S. Dubose
Hattiesburg

Susan Duckworth
Tylertown

Misty D. Duffy
Perkinston

Jason J. Dugas
St. Martinville, LA

Janet M. Dunaway
Foxworth

Anna E. Eiserloh
New Orleans, LA

Martha K. Ekornes
Picayune

Taffanie L. Ellis
Picayune

Tonya M. Ellis
Carriere

Ometricia A. Ellzey
Tylertown

Jesse B. Elmore, III
Foxworth

Stephen M. Elmore
Poplarville

Candace Emerick
Bay St. Louis

Carrie L. English
Picayune

Brenda F. Entrekin
Purvis

Daniel L. Entrekin
Lumberton

Lisa K. Entrekin
Lumberton

Loretta L. Entrekin
Poplarville

Brian K. Ervin
Picayune

Charmaine Espenschied
Lumberton

Jeanette L. Eaque
Nicholson

Lisa M. Eure
Hattiesburg

Lindsey Evans
Hattiesburg

Maria H. Evans
Poplarville

Octavia D. Evans
Picayune

Timothy G. Everett
Sumrall

Clay E. Expose
Columbia

Brian J. Ezell
Lumberton

Terry P. Ezell
Lumberton

Aimee A. Faggard
Lumberton

Donald D. Fail
Picayune

Chris D. Failla
Picayune

Jason W. Fairchild
Poplarville

Paula Fairley
Hattiesburg

Carmen M. Famularo
Picayune

Rebecca D. Famularo
Picayune

Clayton A. Farmer
Poplarville

Robert A. Farrell
Picayune

Sally A. Farris
Columbia

Barbara A. Favaloro
Picayune

Eric D. Favre
Bay St. Louis

Jamie M. Favre
Bay St. Louis

Lawrence J. Favre
Bay St. Louis

Jeanine M. Federowski
Columbia

Teri R. Feeley
Picayune

John Z. Felder, II
Waveland

Mary D. Fell
Slidell, LA

Jane K. Fendlason
Bogalusa, LA

Suzanne R. Fendley
Picayune

Tara F. Ferguson
Picayune

Valerica D. Ferrell
Picayune

Jennifer H. Ferrill
Poplarville

John H. Ferrill
Poplarville

Julie D. Ferrill
Poplarville

Kraig E. Ficken
Picayune

Nathan W. Ficken
Picayune

Daniel P. Finnan
Picayune

Dale E. Firmin
Poplarville

Vernon C. Fisher
Picayune

Leisha M. Flemina
Nicholson

Jan L. Fletcher, Jr.
Bay St. Louis

Tiana M. Flickinger
Bay St. Louis

Mary A. Flood
Poplarville

Janice L. Floyd
Hattiesburg

Barry J. Foil
Picayune

Debra C. Foil
Picayune

Tonya I. Foil
Bogalusa, LA

Tina M. Folse
Poplarville

Sherri L. Foote
Hattiesburg

Pamela Sue Forbes
Carriere

Tonya L. Forbes
Columbia

Lea A. Ford
Poplarville

Stuart D. Fore
Hattiesburg

Sheri G. Fornea
Sandy Hook

Catherine E. Forrest
Bay St. Louis

Murray A. Forsman
Carriere

Gail L. Fortenberry
Picayune

Jerry A. Fortenberry
Columbia

Sheila S. Fortenberry
Angie, LA

Tim C. Fortenberry
Foxworth

Sabrina R. Fortner
Hattiesburg

Linda J. Foster
Poplarville

Mamie L. Fowler
Poplarville

Markal G. Fowler
Purvis

Rico C. Foxworth
Foxworth

Sarah Francabandera
Waveland

Gia M. Franklin
Columbia

Cindy L. Franzen
Bay St. Louis

Tina L. Franzen
Bay St. Louis

Donna C. Frazier
Carriere

Carolyn A. Freeman
Hattiesburg

Gloria D. Freeman
Bogalusa, LA

Stacey L. Freeman
Poplarville

Robert L. French
Farmerville, LA

Ronald J. Frey
Slidell, LA

William R. Fricke
Pearlington

Cynthia D. Frierson
Picayune

Emmy B. Frierson
Picayune

Billy W. Frierson, Jr.
Picayune

Leah D. Frierson
Picayune

Martin G. Frings
Waveland

Alice E. Fulcher
Carriere

Jennifer E. Fuller
Poplarville

Roxanne L. Furey
Pearlington

Hollis Furr
Picayune

Claude S. Gaines
Agnie, LA

Ginnie L. Galloway
Lumberton

Dolores T. Gamble
Picayune

Sharon R. Gandy
Picayune

Betty M. Gardner
Picayune

Donna B. Gardner
Foxworth

Thomas F. Gardner, Jr.
Carriere

J.L. Garner
Foxworth

Corinna M. Garretson
Picayune

Elaine Garrett
Picayune

Francis A. Garrett
Picayune

Jenny M. Garrett
Picayune

Tammy Garrick
Poplarville

Joy B. Garza
Poplarville

Chester J. Gasper
Picayune

Diana L. Gaude
Picayune

Peter B. Gaude
Picayune

Anna R. Gaule
Carriere

Jeannine M. Gauthier
Bay St. Louis

Robin M. Gay
Lumberton

Richard Geeston
Columbia

Daryl R. Geiger
Poplarville

Anthony J. Gendusa
Poplarville

Jacqueline N. Georgia
Lumberton

Patrece L. Georgia
Lumberton

Patricia J. Gerald
Richton

Shenna R. Gerald
Picayune

R. Louis Gholar
Hattiesburg

Mary A. Gibbons
Picayune

Anna D. Gibson
Carriere

Jennifer L. Gibson
Picayune

Tammy R. Gibson
Brooklyn

Tyrance Gilbert
Hattiesburg

Rebecca Gill
Poplarville

Camille L. Gilmore
Picayune

Valerie K. Gilmore
Columbia

Lynn M. Gilreath
Picayune

John P. Gipson
Purvis

Sue L. Gipson
Poplarville

Susan L. Gipson
Lumberton

Patricia G. Glass
Picayune

Sheila A. Godbolt
Hattiesburg

Lucille Golemon
Carriere

Michelle R. Golemon
Carriere

Steven D. Golemon
Carriere

Dennis L. Good, Jr.
Pearlington

Gladys C. Gore
Picayune

Gina M. Goudy
Hattiesburg

Melissa A. Graeter
Poplarville

Tony G. Graeter
Picayune

Donna M. Graham
Foxworth

Franklin J. Graham
Picayune

Janice M. Graham
Poplarville

Mark L. Graham
Columbia

Kerry L. Grant
Poplarville

Phillip A. Grantier
Pass Christian

Vanessa M. Harrell
Carriere

Candice T. Harriel
Perkinston

Karen K. Harriel
Poplarville

Angela K. Harris
Foxworth

Danny Harris
Picayune

Donna J. Harris
Sumrall

Linda L. Harris
Picayune

Myron L. Harris, Jr.
Poplarville

Scott W. Harris
McNeill

Charles R. Harrison
Columbia

Laura L. Harry
Sandy Hook

Leticia O. Harry
Picayune

Craig D. Hart
Poplarville

Cynthia S. Hartfield
Purvis

Rebecca L. Hartfield
Hattiesburg

Karen Hartzog
Picayune

Cindy L. Harvey
Picayune

David J. Hathorn
Columbia

Debra A. Hathorn
Prentiss

Deanna D. Hathorne
Franklinton, LA

Christina M. Hatten
Poplarville

Timothy L. Hatten
Purvis

Todd A. Hatten
Sumrall

Mark M. Haverty
Waveland

Michael L. Haverty
Waveland

Richard J. Hawkins
Waveland

Angela Haynes
Hattiesburg

Libby Heath
Poplarville

Sonia L. Hebert
Poplarville

Kevin W. Hedgepeth
Picayune

Donna F. Henderson
Covington, LA

John D. Henderson
Bogalusa, LA

Marcie A. Henderson
Wiggins

Angela Y. Hendricks
Sumrall

Charline M. Hendrix
Carriere

Russell O. Hendrix
Picayune

Mary A. Henley
Carriere

Flora A. Hennes
Picayune

Eartha T. Henry
Poplarville

Eric J. Henry
Poplarville

Eva M. Henry
Poplarville

Jeannie L. Henry
Poplarville

Mary J. Henry
Poplarville

Mary J. Henry
Poplarville

Mary V. Henry
Lumberton

Norma J. Henry
Poplarville

Phyllis D. Henry
Poplarville

Marsha M. Herman
Picayune

Hilton C. Herndon, Jr.
Poplarville

Josh Herndon
Poplarville

David S. Herrin
Picayune

Loretta Herrin
Sumrall

Robert S. Herrin
Picayune

Alma N. Herrington
Poplarville

Steve K. Hespen
Carriere

Patti L. Hester
Picayune

Tonya N. Hicks
Poplarville

Robert L. Hicks, Jr.
Prentiss

Joe Higginbotham
Nicholson

Paula G. Hilburn
Purvis

Bobbie J. Hill
Carriere

Darold R. Hill
Atlanta, LA

Suzanne R. Hille
Bay St. Louis

Deborah R. Hilton
Picayune

Judith Elaine Hines
Carriere

Archie L. Hinton
Hattiesburg

Lisa S. Hinton
Hattiesburg

Vincent Hinton
Poplarville

Alesia M. Hodgin
Petal

Ivy L. Hodgin
Petal

Suzanne C. Hodnett
Carriere

Jamie L. Hoffmann
Bay St. Louis

Carolyn E. Holcomb
Lumberton

Donna R. Holcomb
Hattiesburg

Eve T. Holland
Poplarville

Nancy J. Holland
Lumberton

Linda K. Hollander
Poplarville

Pamela R. Hollensbe
Picayune

Amy Holliday
Poplarville

Debra A. Hollis
Poplarville

Teresa Holloway
Prentiss

Willie R. Holloway
Columbia

Janice L. Holman
Kokomo

Syble A. Holman
Kokomo

Scott M. Honeychurch
Carriere

Tracy L. Honecutt
Columbia

Keith B. Honomichl
Hattiesburg

Sabrena M. Hooker
Hattiesburg

Charles E. Hopkins
Picayune

Valencia O. Horne
Hattiesburg

Faith B. Houck
Picayune

Helan M. Howard
Poplarville

Kay F. Howard
Carriere

Sheila Marie Howard
Poplarville

Tammy R. Howard
Poplarville

Angela G. Howell
Purvis

Susan S. Howell
Picayune

Frances M. Huck
Picayune

Robert C. Hudson
Hattiesburg

Lisa G. Hughes
Columbia

Patrick Hughes
Bogalusa, LA

Glenn A. Hume
Poplarville

Martha Hume
Poplarville

April R. Humphrey
Poplarville

Barbara G. Hunt
Columbia

Cathy D. Hunt
Poplarville

Pamela L. Hunt
Picayune

Elaine O. Hurlbert
Bay St. Louis

Shirl Hurt
Lumberton

James Hutchins
Prentiss

Terry L. Hutchinson
Bassfield

Jennifer L. Hyatt
Carriere

Kevin T. Ina
Franklin, LA

Charles K. Ingram, Jr.
Sumrall

Karen K. Irvin
Columbia

Bryan W. Jackson
Bassfield

Carl E. Jackson
Poplarville

Cynthia G. Jackson
Picayune

Paulette Jackson
Poplarville

Robert J. Jackson
Gulfport

Edward S. Jacobs
Foxworth

Steven B. Jacobs
Picayune

Marlinda L. James
Poplarville

Lynda Jarrell
Carriere

Miriam P. Jarrell
Poplarville

Pamela A. Jarrell
Carriere

Wendy M. Jarrell
Angie, LA

Mark E. Jeanfreau
Picayune

Latonya A. Jefferson
Angie, LA

David L. Jenkins
Hattiesburg

Linda G. Jenkins
Picayune

Linda L. Jenkins
Carriere

Ulysses Jones
Donaldsonville, LA

Virginia A. Jones
Hattiesburg

Michael Jordan
Hattiesburg

Thelma Y. Jorday
Hattiesburg

Bradley E. Joyce
Carriere

Candice A. Judah
Purvis

Anthony R. Jurich
Picayune

Maryann Keef
Picayune

Teresa L. Keef
Picayune

Chris B. Keith
Purvis

Michael B. Keith
Purvis

Patricia E. Kekko
Picayune

Richard T. Kekko
Carriere

Charles G. Kellar
Picayune

Doyla K. Kellar
Poplarville

Jerry W. Kellar, Jr.
Picayune

Luwanda D. Kellar
Picayune

Stacy L. Kelley
Gulfport

Joseph E. Kelter
Cambridge, WI

Kimberly A. Kendrick
Columbia

Martha Kendrick
Lumberton

Thomas R. Kendrick
Columbia

Cecil A. Kennedy
Picayune

Travis D. Kennedy
Carriere

David R. Kenney
Bogalusa, LA

Ray A. Kent
Hattiesburg

Melanie K. Kerry
Carriere

Jackie G. Keyes
Lumberton

Jerry R. Kihlken, Jr.
Picayune

Brian C. Kimball
Poplarville

Ivory C. Kindred
Hattiesburg

Anthony F. King
Carson

Christopher D. King
Carriere

Kim A. King
Purvis

Leigh W. King
Petal

Sharron L. King
Poplarville

Vivian L. King
Columbia

Wanda T. King
Monticello

Kathleen M. Kinler
Carriere

Randall M. Kipker
Carriere

William G. Kirkland
Carriere

Anthony J. Kite
Poplarville

Stephen C. Klauk
Purvis

Darren M. Kling
Picayune

Buffy M. Knight
Perkinston

Cynthia D. Knight
Hattiesburg

Dennis D. Knight, II
Amite, LA

Ira J. Knight
Columbia

Susan E. Knue
Lumberton

Sharon E. Koenenn
Kiln

Kimberly A. Koenig
Bay St. Louis

Grant W. Kohnke
Bay St. Louis

Owen Kosbab
Waveland

Diane J. Kraft
McNeil

Scott J. Krankey
Bay St. Louis

Willena R. Krekel
Poplarville

Hope E. Kuchler
Nicholson

Margaret Lacavera
Carriere

Christopher Lacoste
Bay St. Louis

Amanda M. Ladner
Pass Christian

Angela D. Ladner
Lumberton

Anissa L. Ladner
Picayune

Camille Ladner
Poplarville

Charnis S. Ladner
Poplarville

Darren H. Ladner
Slidell, LA

Deles E. Ladner
Poplarville

Dianette M. Ladner
Pass Christian

Donald L. Ladner
Picayune

Gail Ladner
Perkinston

Gidget M. Ladner
Poplarville

Greg A. Ladner
Bay St. Louis

James L. Ladner
Picayune

Jason R. Ladner
Columbia

Judith R. Ladner
Poplarville

Kevin M. Ladner
Bay St. Louis

Larrece J. Ladner
Poplarville

Lelie R. Ladner
Bay St. Louis

Marsha D. Ladner
Perkinston

Mary Ladner
Hattiesburg

Natalie C. Ladner
Pass Christian

Norma A. Ladner
Poplarville

Pamela A. Ladner
Lumberton

Pamela M. Ladner
Picayune

Rhett M. Ladner
Pass Christian

Rhonda E. Ladner
Poplarville

Robbie Lander
Poplarville

Roland C. Ladner
Perkinston

Timothy R. Ladner
Poplarville

Tracy Ladner
Poplarville

Virginia A. Ladner
Picayune

Theodore Ladson
Atlanta, GA

Georgia A. Lahti
Bogalusa, LA

Betty E. Laird
Poplarville

Dueal R. Lambert
Columbia

Lori Lancaster
Carriere

Elijah H. Landrum
Lumberton

Kimberly R. Landrum
Poplarville

Donna S. Landry
Purvis

Hughes J. Landry
Picayune

Michael S. Land
Poplarville

Donna B. Langford
Hattiesburg

Jennifer D. Langley
Prentiss

David K. Langnecker
Poplarville

Sharon L. Langston
Picayune

Samantha M. Lansdale
Poplarville

Holly L. Larsen
Picayune

Todd E. Larsen
Picayune

Lon J. Latiolais
St. Martinville, LA

Janice Lavigne
Picayune

Myrtle F. Lavigne
Picayune

Thomas S. Lavigne
Carriere

Charles J. Lavinghouse
Waveland

Stephanie M. Lawless
Bay St. Louis

Jacquelin J. Lawrence
Columbia

Larry W. Lawrence
Poplarville

Linda L. Lazarus
Carriere

Amy C. Lee
Lumberton

Berlon D. Lee
Columbia

Carlyn M. Lee
Picayune

Chris Lee
Picayune

Cindy Lee
McNeill

Cristen L. Lee
Picayune

Dana M. Lee
Picayune

Dona J. Lee
Carriere

Gina G. Lee
Picayune

Jacqueline Y. Lee
Carriere

Judith L. Lee
Poplarville

Kimberly A. Lee
Brooklyn

Norman R. Lee
Picayune

Scott T. Lee
Columbia

Sonya M. Lee
Poplarville

Sonya N. Lee
Picayune

Stephanie D. Lee
Purvis

Stephanie D. Lee
McNeill

Todd A. Lee
Lumberton

Tommy R. Lee
Poplarville

Trudy M. Lee
Picayune

Twyla A. Lee
Picayune

Virginia L. Legg
Lumberton

Carolyn Leggett
Hattiesburg

Jamie M. Lenoir
Picayune

Velma L. Lenoir
Poplarville

Francis A. Leonard
Hattiesburg

Robert H. Leonard
Picayune

Andria Lewis
Poplarville

Anthony S. Lewis
Poplarville

Daniel W. Lewis
Lumberton

Danita J. Lewis
Poplarville

Margret L. Lewis
Lumberton

Melanie J. Lewis
Picayune

Michael D. Lewis
Foxworth

Sabrina R. Lewis
Columbia

Sandra K. Lewis
Carriere

Tony Lewis
Hattiesburg

Lisa D. Lightsey
Foxworth

Deborah M. Lindner
Picayune

June L. Lindsey
Prentiss

Kimberly Lindsey
Lumberton

Michael L. Lindsey
Whistler, AL

Pamela A. Lindsley
Hattiesburg

Jamie A. Lisenbea
Carriere

Lisa A. Little
Poplarville

Melissa A. Liverett
Bay St. Louis

Dennis P. Lizana
Pass Christian

Jeff R. Lockhart, II
Poplarville

Cherry L. Lodrigues
Poplarville

Frances E. Logan
Hattiesburg

Jesse L. Logan
Waveland

Robert C. Longino
Hattiesburg

Derrit T. Loper
Poplarville

Cathy R. Lord
Carriere

Deborah I. Martin
Perkinston

Kimelly B. Martin
Lumberton

Melissa E. Martin
Picayune

Nancy M. Martin
Waveland

Tammy E. Martin
Poplarville

Norris C. Martindale
Picayune

Angela R. Mason
Columbia

Mary A. Mason
Picayune

Jay C. Masoner
Poplarville

Mark D. Masoner
Poplarville

Janice M. Massey
Carriere

Arnold F. Matthews
Picayune

Ernest B. Matthews
Poplarville

Sharon D. Maxwell
Brooklyn

Atlanta M. McDougle
Hattiesburg

Tammy M. McInnis
Lumberton

Karen M. McAllister
Foxworth

Mary M. McBride
Sumrall

Nancy L. McBride
Sumrall

Eva N. McCain
Bogalusa, LA

Regina A. McCall
Picayune

Debbie R. McCardle
Lumberton

Kenneth E. McCardle
Carriere

Rhonda K. McCardle
Lumberton

Samuel C. McCardle
Waveland

Brian K. McCarra
Picayune

Bobbie T. McCarty
Bogalusa, LA

Kimberly J. McClinton
Carriere

Prezel McCloud
Carson

Veronica A. McCollum
Hattiesburg

Berry L. McCormick
Picayune

Michele P. McCormick
Picayune

Jimmy W. McCraw, Jr.
Columbia

Ruby N. McCullum
Hattiesburg

Bridget P. McDaniel
Bogalusa, LA

Shannon E. McDaniel
Columbia

Holly B. McDonald
Lumberton

Lisa E. McDonald
Poplarville

Reuben W. McDowell
Sumrall

Christopher McFarland
Columbia

Edna L. McGee
Picayune

Robert M. McGee
Foxworth

Antrice McGill
Picayune

Melissa T. McGill
Picayune

Robert C. McGinty
Purvis

Erika V. McGowan
Foxworth

Robert F. McGrath, Jr.
Hattiesburg

Angela M. McIntyre
Carriere

Katrina M. McKean
Carriere

Pam R. McKean
Nicholson

Trenda McKee
Picayune

Kristi M. McKenzie
Purvis

Julia C. McKinney
Hattiesburg

Emelie S. McLean
Columbia

Melanie D. McNabb
Columbia

Darrell L. McNair
Prentiss

Terry T. McNeese
Columbia

Ruth E. McNeil
Picayune

Margaret McPherson
Poplarville

Mutt McRaney
Foxworth

Sonya McRaney
Collins

Jamal D. McSwain
Hattiesburg

Shaundra Means
Picayune

Dana L. Meeks
Purvis

Russell A. Meitzler
Picayune

Susan L. Melilli
Carriere

Joseph Mendoza
Bay St. Louis

Shari E. Mendoza
Poplarville

Henry Menner, III
Picayune

Donnetta W. Mensah
Hattiesburg

Marie Merritt
Poplarville

Shirley A. Merritt
Kokomo

Terry G. Merritt
Lumberton

Todd B. Merritt
Lumberton

Mark E. Messmer
Slidell, LA

Scott A. Metzler
Picayune

Douglas J. Michna
Slidell, LA

Chris E. Miciello
Carriere

Nancy T. Miele
Slidell, LA

Sandra P. Miele
Carriere

Randall D. Mikell
Prentiss

Alicia R. Miles
McNeill

Anvia Miller
Poplarville

Blaine Miller
Crowley, LA

Christine M. Miller
Poplarville

Diana Miller
Carriere

Elbert D. Miller
McNeil

Glenn E. Miller
Carriere

Karen E. Miller
Bogalusa, LA

Larry B. Miller
Bogalusa, LA

Margrith A. Miller
Poplarville

Mary L. Miller
Carriere

Nancy B. Miller
Sumrall

Rosemary Miller
Picayune

Shirley L. Miller
Poplarville

Teri J. Miller
Sumrall

Teri M. Miller
Picayune

Kenneth W. Milligan
Picayune

David A. Mills
Carriere

Freddy L. Mills, Jr.
Bassfield

June C. Milner
Poplarville

Chandra K. Minckler
Carriere

Cheri R. Minckler
Carriere

Darlene M. Minton
Bay St. Louis

Amanda K. Mitchell
Picayune

Angelae S. Mitchell
Picayune

Barbara A. Mitchell
Picayune

Betty L. Mitchell
Picayune

Bobby W. Mitchell
Poplarville

Constance D. Mitchell
Picayune

Dawn E. Mitchell
Picayune

Edward E. Mitchell, Jr.
Columbia

Gencie Mitchell
Poplarville

Ketrina B. Mitchell
Richton

Lois J. Mitchell
Picayune

Lydia A. Mitchell
Poplarville

Mary V. Mitchell
Picayune

Hattie L. Morris
Hattiesburg

Jol M. Morris
Poplarville

Leigh S. Morris
Poplarville

Tristessa D. Morris
Jayess

Virginia Morris
Poplarville

Virginia D. Morris
Poplarville

Willie R. Morris
Poplarville

Janne M. Morrison
Lumberton

Dorothy D. Moseley
Bay St. Louis

Glenn Moses
Columbia

Willie W. Moses
Columbia

Anita C. Mosley
Hattiesburg

Benjamin C. Moss
Grand Bay, AL

Judy C. Mozizgo
Lumberton

Jeffrey A. Mullins
Picayune

Jerri S. Mullins
Columbia

Barborah S. Murphree
Picayune

Traci Murphy
Lumberton

Darrell C. Murray
Carriere

Jamie M. Murray
Carriere

Jacqueline D. Myers
Hattiesburg

Myoshia Myers
Picayune

Niki L. Myers
Prentiss

Carolyn S. Myrick
Poplarville

Brandon D. Nace
Kokomo

Mary A. Nanney
Poplarville

Teresa Lynn Nanney
Petal

Joseph D. Napier
Poplarville

Raymond Nash
Sorrento, LA

Valerie E. Nations
Bogalusa, LA

Dewayne S. Nease
DeRidder, LA

Daphne Necaise
Pass Christian

Don C. Necaise
Pass Christian

Greg Necaise
Waveland

Leanne Necaise
Perkinston

Mark W. Necaise
Bay St. Louis

Melissa D. Necaise
Picayune

Michele R. Necaise
Picayune

Sandy S. Necaise
Pass Christian

Thomas C. Necaise
Bay St. Louis

Andrew J. Neely
Atlanta, GA

Angela R. Nelson
Columbia

Candace Nelson
Picayune

Dawn G. Nelson
Poplarville

Earl Nelson, II
Poplarville

William Nelson
Poplarville

Susan R. Nemmers
Lumberton

Robert S. Nestle
Poplarville

Kathryn L. Neves
Purvis

Greta D. Newell
Sumrall

John W. Newell
Picayune

Coy T. Newson
New Hebron

Juan M. Newton
Prentiss

Michael D. Nichelson
Picayune

Eric D. Nixon
Carriere

Chris B. Noble
Carriere

June A. Noble
Carriere

Charles M. Noblitt, Jr.
Pascagoula

Maria K. Nolan
Picayune

Sharon Nonemacher
Lumberton

Myra Norwood
Prentiss

Geraldine Nunn
Purvis

Dorothy M. Nussbaum
Lakeshore

Nathalie L. O'Berry
Poplarville

Abrilla D. Oatis
Basafield

Dick J. Ockman, Jr.
Lumberton

Charlotte M. Odom
Poplarville

George D. Odom
Hattiesburg

John P. Odom
Poplarville

Sandra K. Odom
Lumberton

Sharon A. Odom
Picayune

Synthia Odom
Columbia

Maxine E. Odum
Lumberton

Jeannine A. Oestreich
Kiln

Marc A. Ogden
Purvis

Kirk T. Oge
Bay St. Louis

Timothy R. Oglesby
Petal

Danny B. Oneal
Wiggins

Connie S. Oquin
Foxworth

Janice Osby
Bogalusa, LA

Berwick D. Ostheimer
Oakvale

Pamela G. Overstreet
Lumberton

Karen L. Owens
Poplarville

Lisa M. Owens
Poplarville

Michael L. Owens
Lumberton

Daniel S. Pace
Columbia

Jeff W. Pace
Sumrall

Staci A. Pace
Bogalusa, LA

Victoria Pack
Angie, LA

Goretta D. Page
Hattiesburg

Martha J. Page
Lumberton

Curtis W. Paige
Perkinston

Rebecca M. Palmer
Picayune

Leslie A. Pardue
Lumberton

Robert S. Parish
Sumrall

Gretchen N. Parker
Picayune

Lashawn Parker
Purvis

Theodore Parson
Poplarville

Charlene P. Partridge
Carriere

Meena Patel
Columbia

Dawn M. Patterson
Sumrall

Shannon L. Patterson
Sumrall

Joseph Paylor
Hattiesburg

Anita D. Payton
Picayune

Alan Peacock
Hattiesburg

Donna G. Pearson
Carriere

Todd A. Pearson
Carriere

Edith Pedescleaux
Donaldsonville, LA

Belinda H. Pellegrin
Poplarville

Chester V. Pendowski
Foxworth

Jolina Pennington
Hattiesburg

Charles E. Penton
Pearl River, LA

Connie F. Penton
Picayune

Connie S. Penton
Picayune

Dennis Penton
Carriere

Shelley C. Penton
Picayune

Thelma L. Penton
Pearl River, LA

Karin L. Pepiton
Picayune

Ronnie J. Percy
Poplarville

Kathleen J. Perry
Carriere

Sharon A. Peters
Poplarville

Rebecca S. Peterson
Perkinston

Ryan S. Peterson
Pass Christian

Scott D. Peterson
Perkinston

Cynthia J. Phelps
Picayune

Kimberly A. Phillips
Poplarville

Mary E. Phillips
Lumberton

James R. Philyaw
Carriere

259

Valencia C. Pichon
Poplarville

William H. Pickering
Picayune

Deidre A. Pickett
Sumrall

Christopher Pierce
Picayune

Tammy L. Piercy
Hattiesburg

Jeffrey Pigott
Slidell, LA

Andrea V. Piper
Picayune

Angela Pittman
Picayune

Anita K. Pittman
Foxworth

Jennifer D. Pittman
Columbia

Katrena A. Pittman
Sandy Hook

Paulette Pittman
Poplarville

Richard Pittman
Columbia

Roderick Pittman
Poplarville

Stacy L. Pittman
Hattiesburg

Toni Pittman
Poplarville

J. Adriel Poche
Perkinston

Theresa L. Poche
Perkinston

William M. Poche
Baton Rouge, LA

Kevin B. Polk
Hattiesburg

Margaret Pollock
Lumberton

Janice M. Poole
Poplarville

Wayne K. Pope
Columbia

Frank E. Pounds
Columbia

Janet E. Pounds
Foxworth

John M. Pounds
Foxworth

Melody K. Pounds
Poplarville

Sherman L. Pounds
Foxworth

Tammy L. Pounds
Bogalusa, LA

Wendy K. Pounds
Foxworth

James R. Powe
Carriere

Linda S. Powe
Poplarville

Amie K. Powell
Foxworth

Juli R. Powell
Foxworth

Paul W. Powell
Petal

Suzanne Powell
Columbia

Terry L. Powell
Foxworth

William J. Power, III
Waveland

Tommy L. Prather
Brooklyn

William E. Prather
Picayune

Vanessa A. Preston
Columbia

Karen A. Prewett
Picayune

Cathy A. Price
Picayune

Sharon D. Price
Poplarville

Randy Prince
Carriere

Sandra Prince
Poplarville

Sandra C. Prine
Hattiesburg

Greg T. Pritchett
Poplarville

Velina Pryor
Picayune

Janice M. Pucheu
Kiln

Michael R. Pugh
Picayune

Marcia L. Pullen
Lumberton

Rebecca L. Pullen
Poplarville

Judy L. Pullens
Carriere

Marty J. Pulliam
Petal

Ruth A. Pulsifer
Kiln

Charlene R. Purdy
Bay St. Louis

Robert R. Purvis, Jr.
Bogalusa, LA

Kenneth W. Putnam
Carriere

Anne T. Raborn
Columbia

Bryan L. Raby
Nicholson

Clayton B. Raine
Poplarville

Ladonna D. Raine
Poplarville

Tomeka B. Raine
Poplarville

Carla J. Raines
Carriere

Katherine A. Raines
Picayune

Daniel D. Raisor
Hattiesburg

James S. Ramsay
Carriere

Shonda R. Ramsey
Bogalusa, LA

Betty Ramshur
Picayune

Lisa M. Ramshur
Columbia

Danielle R. Randell
Poplarville

Bryan C. Rankin
Lumberton

Michael L. Raphael
Bay St. Louis

Frances D. Rawls
Poplarville

Samuel L. Rawls
Picayune

Lisa Ray
Pearlington

Montell Ray
Purvis

Tanya R. Rayborn
Lumberton

Glenn D. Rayburn
Slidell, LA

Jeffery T. Rayburn
Carriere

James M. Raziano
Poplarville

Joey A. Reagan
Kokomo

Alma L. Recatto
McNeil

Leslie Reddick
Poplarville

Martin E. Reddick
Foxworth

Wanda J. Reddick
Poplarville

Jerry C. Reed
Carson

Tracie A. Reed
Bay St. Louis

Stacy Reese
Picayune

Tommy Reese
Picayune

Frances E. Reeves
Pass Christian

Timothy J. Reeves
Picayune

Donald A. Regan
Columbia

Debbie A. Reid
Lumberton

Eric S. Reid
Lumberton

Jon A. Reid
Poplarville

Larry M. Reid
Lumberton

Lee A. Reid
Columbia

Linda J. Reid
Lumberton

Peggy E. Reid
Lumberton

Rhonda J. Reid
Columbia

Rhonda K. Reid
Lumberton

Shawna L. Reid
Poplarville

Judy R. Reinholtz
Picayune

Tiffany R. Renfro
Bay St. Louis

Edward R. Rensch
Metairie, LA

Curtis Rester
Lumberton

Mary C. Rester
Poplarville

Patricia L. Rester
Poplarville

Peggy J. Rester
Poplarville

Wade Rester
Pearl River, LA

Lori A. Reyer
Poplarville

Virginia A. Reyer
Poplarville

Diane E. Reynolds
Bay St. Louis

Paul B. Reynolds
Lumberton

Charles J. Rhodes
Bay St. Louis

Michelle E. Rice
Purvis

Katrina L. Richard
Picayune

Donna G. Richardson
Ponchatoula, LA

Jerri D. Richardson
Lumberton

Kathleen Richardson
Poplarville

Linda Ricks
Carriere

Lenora T. Rifai
Picayune

Gail C. Riggins
Poplarville

Mark A. Rigney
Poplarville

Tabitha G. Riley
Columbia

Daniel L. Ris
Poplarville

Michael R. Risley
Kiln

Thompson M. Rivers
Picayune

Charles L. Roberson
Carriere

Joy L. Roberson
Mandeville, LA

Merina R. Roberson
Bay St. Louis

James J. Roberts
Slidell, LA

Kenneth D. Roberts
Picayune

Michelle V. Roberts
Picayune

Wendy H. Roberts
Lumberton

Greg A. Robertson
Morgantown

Wesley B. Robertson
Carriere

Roderick D. Robertson
Bay St. Louis

Sena M. Robertson
Poplarville

Sulvester J. Robertson
Picayune

Kimberly A. Robichaux
Columbia

Chris M. Robin
Broussard, LA

Brandi Robinson
Picayune

Charles F. Robinson
Picayune

Cynthia R. Robinson
Picayune

Donald Robinson
Poplarville

Ronald Robinson
Poplarville

Senta J. Robinson
Picayune

Steven C. Robinson
Hattiesburg

Temekia L. Robinson
Carriere

Vicki R. Robinson
Columbia

Sheila L. Robnett
Wiggins

Lisa M. Roche
Carriere

Eric R. Rocker
Poplarville

Annette Rogers
Hattiesburg

Michael C. Rogers
Picayune

Pricella Rogers
Hattiesburg

Steven P. Rogers
Picayune

Delee L. Samford
Bogalusa, LA

Andrew Samples
Picayune

Jeffery S. Samples
Picayune

Deborah S. Sampson
Picayune

Rodney E. Sampson
Picayune

Carl Sanders
Hattiesburg

Helen E. Sanders
Petal

Christine Sandifer
Lumberton

Randy D. Sanford
Carriere

Mary R. Sargent
Purvis

Angelina A. Saucier
Brooklyn

Clint A. Saucier
Lumberton

Deanna G. Saucier
Lumberton

Jane G. Saucier
Poplarville

John F. Saucier
Poplarville

Kelvin E. Saucier
Poplarville

Kim A. Saucier
Purvis

Gary M. Savelle
Carriere

Davey W. Scarborough
Wiggins

Richard C. Shaefer
Lumberton

Lynn A. Schaller
Nicholson

Lisa M. Schielder
Picayune

Sheree C. Schilling
Bogalusa, LA

Jodie M. Schmidt
Metairie, LA

Malter C. Scobel
Bay St. Louis

Slint Scott
Poplarville

Dedra D. Scott
Hattiesburg

Johnny L. Scott
Hattiesburg

Joyce A. Scott
Carriere

Martha L. Scott
Carriere

Shelly Scott
Carriere

Karla W. Scruggs
Carriere

Charles G. Seal
Picayune

Edward B. Seal
Carriere

Hannah M. Seal
Poplarville

Jenny L. Seal
Poplarville

Kimber L. Seal
Bogalusa, LA

Michael R. Seal
Picayune

Robin F. Seal
Pass Christian

Sarah L. Seal
Picayune

Susan E. Seal
Picayune

Norma J. Seals
Franklinton, LA

Rebecca Seals
Poplarville

Calvin L. Seaton
Bogalusa, LA

Debra A. Sechrengost
Picayune

Thomas E. Selby
Picayune

Gregory A. Selg
Slidell, LA

Vicki M. Seligman
Poplarville

Evelyn P. Sellers
Purvis

Traci A. Selman
Columbia

Edward S. Semmes
Picayune

Jack D. Sessions
Pearlington

Marilyn A. Sevin
Poplarville

Carolyn S. Sharp
Crossroads

Jacquelyn S. Sharp
Bogalusa, LA

Phillip R. Shaw
Perkinston

Ratonia L. Shaw
Hattiesburg

Roy M. Shaw
Perkinston

Vincent B. Shelton
Hattiesburg

Cedric Sheridan
Columbia

Steffi L. Sheridan
Bogalusa, LA

Debra A. Shields
Picayune

Ladonna M. Shiyou
Pass Christian

Kathi Short
Poplarville

Charlotte Silas
Poplarville

Charzes D. Silas
Hattiesburg

Carolyn E. Simmons
Bogalusa, LA

Rena C. Simmons
Hattiesburg

Sherry K. Simmons
Purvis

Mike Simms
Hattiesburg

Clemar J. Simon
Hattiesburg

Tina M. Simpson
Poplarville

Deborah G. Singley
Columbia

Judy L. Sistrunk
Foxworth

Clarice A. Skipper
Picayune

Jeanne C. Slade
Poplarville

Charles D. Slater
Picayune

William E. Slaven
Amite, LA

Douglas H. Slocum
Kokomo

Lana G. Small
Poplarville

Regina C. Small
Poplarville

Sngela D. Smith
Poplarville

Angela J. Smith
Sumrall

Aniesa Smith
Poplarville

Ann E. Smith
Perkinston

Bertha A. Smith
Angie, LA

Bobby R. Smith
Slidell, LA

Bonnie E. Smith
Picayune

Cynthia T. Smith
Carriere

Deborah A. Smith
Hattiesburg

Donna A. Smith
Poplarville

Dorothy F. Smith
Carriere

Douglas R. Smith
Poplarville

Drew T. Smith
Perkinston

Harvel Smith
Hattiesburg

James L. Smith
Picayune

Jeannie R. Smith
Poplarville

Jeff R. Smith
Slidell, LA

Jeptha E. Smith
Poplarville

John M. Smith
Hattiesburg

John P. Smith
Foxworth

Karen J. Smith
Picayune

Karla K. Smith
Picayune

Kenneth M. Smith
Lumberton

Leslie R. Smith
Lumberton

Lillie B. Smith
Lumberton

Marla N. Smith
Hattiesburg

Martin B. Smith
Poplarville

Marvin K. Smith
Harvey, LA

Mildred M. Smith
Carriere

Paulette Smith
Picayune

Rafe L. Smith
Poplarville

Rhonda J. Smith
Poplarville

Robert W. Smith
Poplarville

Sheila R. Smith
Poplarville

Sherri M. Smith
Bay St. Louis

Shirley M. Smith
Picayune

Sonya G. Smith
Poplarville

Steven C. Smith
Poplarville

Stewart R. Smith
Poplarville

Suzanne E. Smith
Hattiesburg

T. Glenn Smith
Picayune

Tammy R. Smith
Poplarville

Teresa Smith
Poplarville

Therman S. Smith
Carriere

Vicki L. Smith
Picayune

Wanda K. Smith
Columbia

Wendi A. Smith
Carriere

William C. Smith
Picayune

Cindy L. Snapp
Picayune

David S. Snow
Amite, LA

Regina K. Sones
McNeil

Richard M. Sones
Columbia

Tammy J. Sones
Poplarville

Ursula Spanks
Picayune

Linda K. Speed
Hattiesburg

Pamela M. Speights
Newhebron

Robert E. Speights
Bassfield

Tamara L. Speights
Bogalusa, LA

David R. Spence
Carriere

Steven J. Spence
Carriere

Alice L. Spiers
McNeill

Charlotte A. Spiers
Carriere

Donna S. Spiers
Carriere

Jennifer A. Spiers
Poplarville

Raymond D. Spiers
Carriere

Rhonda R. Spiers
Picayune

William T. Spiers
Picayune

Joseph P. Spino, III
Violet, LA

Daren T. St. Amant
Mandeville, LA

Kimberly A. St. Romain
Poplarville

Pamela A. St. Romain
Columbia

Mason R. Stafford
Carriere

Catherine C. Stanford
Poplarville

Crisper H. Stanford
Poplarville

Russell Stanley
Hattiesburg

Susan M. Staples
Nicholson

Melody A. Starr
Bay St. Louis

Melissa G. Steed
Petal

Keith R. Steele
Hattiesburg

Stephen S. Steelman
Picayune

Kirk A. Stenklyft
Cambridge, WI

Jeneanne P. Stephens
Poplarville

Paul L. Stephens
Petal

Robert M. Sterling
Lumberton

Janice C. Stevens
Picayune

Samantha R. Stevens
Picayune

Jeffery A. Stevenson
Picayune

Brian D. Stewart
Columbia

Felix E. Stewart, Jr.
Mobile, AL

James C. Stewart
Poplarville

Johnnie S. Stewart
Carriere

Sandra S. Stewart
Bogalusa, LA

Scott R. Stewart
Poplarville

Sharon E. Stewart
Carriere

Kellie A. Stillwell
Poplarville

Shirley A. Stockman
Poplarville

Betty J. Stockstill
Picayune

Bridget A. Stockstill
Picayune

Carey A. Stockstill
Carriere

Jackie Stockstill
Picayune

James D. Stockstill, III
Picayune

James W. Stockstill, Jr.
Picayune

Kelley Stockstill
Picayune

Laurie A. Stockstill
Picayune

Marcus S. Stockstill
Picayune

Rachelle J. Stockstill
Picayune

Richard S. Stockstill
Carriere

Rickey Stockstill
Picayune

Sarah L. Stockstill
Picayune

T. Joyce Stockstill
Picayune

Timothy L. Stockstill
Carriere

W.D. Stockstill, Jr.
Picayune

Peggy Stogner
Foxworth

Sharon S. Stogner
Poplarville

Thomas W. Strahan
Poplarville

Tammy M. Strain
Carriere

Nancy Stravinsky
Carriere

Anastasia Strimel
Hattiesburg

Denise R. Stringer
Foxworth

Gwen Stringer
Prentiss

John M. Stringer
Foxworth

Ques E. Stringer
Columbia

Sandra K. Stringer
Foxworth

Brenda S. Stringfellow
Lumberton

Janis R. Stringfield
Columbia

David J. Stromeyer
Metairie, LA

Monty Strong
Bay St. Louis

Neil Struppa
Hattiesburg

Deborah S. Stuart
Purvis

Kerri S. Stuart
Picayune

Terry Stuart
Bogalusa, LA

Steven C. Stubbs
Picayune

Sunny J. Stubbs
Picayune

Linda M. Stuckey
Columbia

Scott J. Suhor
Picayune

Trevor K. Summers
Picayune

Ernest Sumrall
Poplarville

James D. Sumrall
Franklinton, LA

Kenneth W. Sumrall
Sumrall

Mary K. Sumrall
Folsom, LA

Robert C. Swearingen
Petal

Shawna D. Swilley
Lumberton

Carla M. Swindle
Picayune

Christy L. Sylvest
Picayune

Michael L. Tagert
Columbia

Johnny L. Tart
Hattiesburg

Scott N. Tartavoulle
Bay St. Louis

Jason Tarver
Winnfield, LA

Zelda D. Tarvin
Hattiesburg

Steven L. Tate
Purvis

Althea M. Tavai
Lumberton

Sondray P. Taylor
Picayune

Sherrie M. Teck
Purvis

Irvin F. Temple
Carriere

Laurie J. Terrell
Foxworth

David M. Terry
Columbia

Kimberly A. Terry
Columbia

Anna M. Thaxton
Carriere

Carol L. Thigpen
Picayune

Mary S. Thigpen
Picayune

Edda Thomas
Purvis

Ernie M. Thomas
Picayune

Louis A. Thomas, IV
Picayune

Shana Thomas
Franklinton, LA

Theodore Thomas
Denham Springs, LA

Zina M. Thomas
Poplarville

Anita L. Thompson
Bassfield

Barbara I. Thompson
Columbia

Charles E. Thompson
Columbia

Earnest L. Thompson
Bassfield

Jenel Thompson
Foxworth

Linda C. Thompson
Picayune

Richard T. Thompson
Bassfield

Ronald J. Thompson
Picayune

Stephen B. Thompson
Bassfield

Terry J. Thompson
Petal

Shawn K. Thornhill
Columbia

Dusbone Tillman
Carriere

Regina M. Tippit
Foxworth

Jamie L. Todd
Sumrall

Melissa Y. Todd
Hattiesburg

Sandra J. Todd
Picayune

James R. Tolar
Oakvale

Nancy A. Tolar
Columbia

Regina K. Tolar
Sumrall

Donnie L. Toney
Brooklyn

Steven C. Toney
Poplarville

Cindy S. Touchstone
Sumrall

Stacy T. Townsend
Lumberton

Andrew M. Tracey
Pearl River, LA

Paige I. Tracey
Pearl River, LA

Sandy Trahan
Poplarville

Sherie D. Travis
Poplarville

Dora E. Treech
Picayune

Josephus Tribbett
Picayune

Kimberly D. Trimble
Poplarville

Jeanene Trotter
Poplarville

Mary L. Trotter
Poplarville

Stephen L. Trotter
McNeill

Billy Trusley
Picayune

Brad A. Trussell
Hattiesburg

Joseph W. Turnage
Foxworth

Kenneth R. Turnage
Foxworth

Bobbie J. Turner
Hattiesburg

Ladonna D. Turner
Poplarville

Herron L. Turnipseed
Bay St. Louis

Nathalie A. Turnpaugh
Carriere

Carmen D. Walker
Picayune

John H. Walker
Picayune

Ronald W. Walker
Angie, LA

Sarah A. Walker
Hattiesburg

Shawn M. Walker
Sumrall

Amy L. Wallace
Picayune

Ronny M. Wallace
McNeill

Tina M. Wallace
Picayune

Ronnie T. Waller
Columbia

Melinda K. Walley
Brooklyn

Twila Walters
Hattiesburg

Delinda Waltmon
Columbia

Alonza A. Ward
Hattiesburg

Kyle D. Ward
Baton Rouge, LA

Maria M. Ward
Columbia

Steve A. Ward
Hattiesburg

Robert D. Ware
Poplarville

Jason K. Warren
Hattiesburg

Lisa D. Warren
Sumrall

Horace Washington
Covington, LA

Sedrick N. Washington
Prentiss

Janelle Watkins
Nicholson

Kerri M. Watkins
Hattiesburg

Chris L. Watts
Hattiesburg

Mark A. Watts
Columbia

Melanie A. Watts
Picayune

Robette M. Watts
Picayune

Adrian Weathersby
Newhebron

Reginald D. Weathersby
Newhebron

Andrea L. Webb
Picayune

Mark A. Wedig
Carriere

Michael C. Weems
Bay St. Louis

Kimberly D. Wells
Carriere

Mackie R. Wells
Poplarville

Mary S. Wells
Poplarville

Tamala L. Wells
Hattiesburg

Robert D. Welsh
Carriere

Charles A. Wesley
Poplarville

Connie S. West
Carriere

Joseph B. West
Bassfield

Mary E. West
Picayune

Norman D. West
Picayune

Larissa D. Westbrook
Picayune

Judy C. Westfaul
Brooklyn

John D. Whatley
Brooklyn

Darron D. Wheat
Purvis

Keith H. Wheeler
Carriere

Lynda K. Whipple
Lumberton

Diana L. Whisnant
Poplarville

Aaron Thomas White
Columbia

Geraldine White
Hattiesburg

Jacqueline L. White
Poplarville

James E. White
Poplarville

Lauri L. White
Lumberton

Mirium F. White
Bay St. Louis

Robert White
Picayune

Larry W. Whitehead
Foxworth

Yolanda C. Whitehead
Picayune

Harold Whiteman, Jr.
Lumberton

Corine C. Whitfield
Carriere

Jackie L. Whitfield
Picayune

Tara M. Whitfield
McNeill

Sharon C. Whittington
Mandeville, LA

Carla G. Wilkerson
Carriere

John D. Wilkinson
Picayune

Michael J. Wilkinson
Picayune

Millie R. Wilks
Columbia

Andrea C. Williams
Picayune

Anthony J. Williams
Hattiesburg

Carol C. Williams
Poplarville

Deloris Williams
Hattiesburg

Donna M. Williams
Sumrall

James A. Williams
Poplarville

Joseph A. Williams
Poplarville

Rita J. Williams
Carriere

Susan J. Williams
Picayune

Terry Williams
Picayune

Billy A. Williamson
Sumrall

Earnest M. Williamson
Sumrall

Linda A. Williamson
Purvis

Marsha Williamson
Purvis

Theresa A. Williamson
Picayune

Tracy L. Williford
Lumberton

Kimberly S. Willis
Picayune

Lisa Y. Willis
Hattiesburg

Tracie L. Willis
Bogalusa, LA

Barbara Willoughby
Picayune

Drake Willoughby
Columbia

Margaret J. Willoughby
Poplarville

Wendy K. Willoughby
Picayune

Barbara A. Wilson
Perkinston

Gale Wilson
Picayune

James A. Wilson
Bassfield

Kelly L. Wilson
Bassfield

Lisa S. Wilson
Perkinston

Patricia V. Wilson
Poplarville

Rodney A. Wilson, Jr.
Picayune

Stokley Wilson
Hattiesburg

Barbara A. Wise
Poplarville

Margaret A. Wise
Poplarville

Melissa D. Wise
Picayune

Roxanne M. Wise
Carriere

William B. Witsell
Poplarville

Mack E. Womack
Newhebron

Shelly Womack
Newhebron

Jerry P. Wood
Pearlington

Pamela K. Wood
Picayune

Rebecca G. Wood
Poplarville

Jimmy M. Woodwurn
Picayune

Joseph B. Woods
Bay St. Louis

Lucretia A. Woodson
Poplarville

Earl J. Wooten
Carriere

Fredrick E. Worthy
Prentiss

Michelle B. Wright
Hattiesburg

Patcy Wright
Bay St. Louis

Gary J. Wyman, Jr.
Pearlington

Arthur D. Wynne, III
New Orleans, LA

Ellen Wynne
New Orleans, LA

John B. Yates, Jr.
Sumrall

Bridgette A. Young
Purvis

Darlene M. Young
Hattiesburg

David W. Young, Jr.
Foxworth

Elizabeth A. Young
Columbia

James T. Young, Jr.
Carriere

Rosa L. Young
Poplarville

Emanuel Zanders, III
Amite, LA

Carl M. Zoll
Poplarville

Lightning Source UK Ltd.
Milton Keynes UK
UKHW022231140219
337291UK00006B/179/P